BUSY
IDIOTS

BUSY IDIOTS

Learn the Brain Science and Productivity Hacks to Get Ahead without the Stress

BRAD MARSHALL
JOFF OUTLAW

WILEY

First published 2025 by John Wiley & Sons Australia, Ltd

© Bradley Joseph Marshall and Jonathan Outlaw 2025

All rights reserved, including rights for text and data mining and training of artificial intelligence technologies or similar technologies. Except as permitted under *the Australian Copyright Act 1968* (for example, a fair dealing for the purposes of study, research, criticism or review) no part of this publication may be reproduced, stored in a retrieval system, or transmitted, in any form or by any means, electronic, mechanical, photocopying, recording or otherwise. Advice on how to obtain permission to reuse material from this title is available at http://www.wiley.com/go/permissions.

The right of Bradley Joseph Marshall and Jonathan Outlaw to be identified as the authors of *Busy Idiots* has been asserted in accordance with law.

ISBN: 978-1-394-28272-2

A catalogue record for this book is available from the National Library of Australia

Registered Office
John Wiley & Sons Australia, Ltd. Level 4, 600 Bourke Street, Melbourne, VIC 3000, Australia

For details of our global editorial offices, customer services, and more information about Wiley products visit us at www.wiley.com.

Wiley also publishes its books in a variety of electronic formats and by print-on-demand. Some content that appears in standard print versions of this book may not be available in other formats.

Trademarks: Wiley and the Wiley logo are trademarks or registered trademarks of John Wiley & Sons, Inc. and/or its affiliates in the United States and other countries and may not be used without written permission. All other trademarks are the property of their respective owners. John Wiley & Sons, Inc. is not associated with any product or vendor mentioned in this book.

Limit of Liability/Disclaimer of Warranty
While the publisher and authors have used their best efforts in preparing this work, they make no representations or warranties with respect to the accuracy or completeness of the contents of this work and specifically disclaim all warranties, including without limitation any implied warranties of merchantability or fitness for a particular purpose. No warranty may be created or extended by sales representatives, written sales materials or promotional statements for this work. This work is sold with the understanding that the publisher is not engaged in rendering professional services. The advice and strategies contained herein may not be suitable for your situation. You should consult with a specialist where appropriate. The fact that an organisation, website, or product is referred to in this work as a citation and/or potential source of further information does not mean that the publisher and authors endorse the information or services the organisation, website, or product may provide or recommendations it may make. Further, readers should be aware that websites listed in this work may have changed or disappeared between when this work was written and when it is read. Neither the publisher nor authors shall be liable for any loss of profit or any other commercial damages, including but not limited to special, incidental, consequential, or other damages.

Cover and internal people images: © Anna Semenchenko/Getty Images, © Zdenek Sasek/Adobe Stock
Cover and internal author photos: Isaac Smith
Lightbulb illustration: © Kebon doodle/Adobe Stock
Cover design by Wiley

Set in Warnock Pro 12/16pt by Straive, Chennai, India
Printed and bound by CPI Group (UK) Ltd, Croydon, CR0 4YY

C9781394282722_221024

Busyness, or rather our obsession with busyness, is the biggest, yet still unspoken issue in the modern workplace.

Contents

About the authors — *ix*

Acknowledgements — *xi*

Introduction: What/who is a Busy Idiot? — *xiii*

Part I: Manage your tech — **1**

1 How did we get so goddamn busy? — 3

2 How to stop bouncing around like a Busy Idiot — 19

Part II: Manage your work and family life — **39**

3 How to manage your busy boss — 41

4 The challenges of loneliness and disconnection — 85

5 You can't go it alone: how to form productive teams — 97

6 Family life: work to live or live to work — it's your call — 141

Conclusion: Imagine a world free of Busy Idiots? — *159*

Get in touch — *165*

References — *167*

About
the authors

Brad Marshall and Joff Outlaw have been friends for over a decade. Together, they help some of the world's best-known companies to increase their organisational productivity and employee happiness by combining psychology with real-world business insights. Through their high-energy speaking and workshop facilitation, they prove that work doesn't have to be miserable. They are on a mission to put an end to the corporate love affair with busyness.

Brad Marshall

B.A. Psych; M.Beh.Sci; M.Res; PhD candidate

Brad is an internationally published author, speaker and workshop facilitator, psychologist and researcher. His previous books, *How to Say No to Your Phone* and *The Tech Diet for Your Child & Teen*, have been published in more than a dozen countries and multiple languages. But it's his clinical experience that sets him apart from other speakers in the field of healthy tech use, productivity and connection. While others speak about research and hypotheticals, Brad delivers from a place of deep real-world experience, drawing on 15 years as Director of the Screens and Gaming Disorder Clinic in Sydney, Australia.

Brad is a thought leader who enjoys cutting through 'psycho-babble' jargon to help his audience to harvest technology and not let technology harvest them. He is passionate about the neuroscience around loneliness and the need for real connection in this disconnected and lonely modern world.

Joff Outlaw

BA Hons English and History

Joff Outlaw is a seasoned business leader with over two decades of experience in digital and technology consulting, having made significant contributions to the industry in the UK and Australia. During a distinguished career Joff has been associated with some of the world's largest technology and management consultancies, including Accenture, PwC and Wipro. As the A/NZ Managing Director of Designit, one of the world's largest strategic design agencies, Joff has shaped innovative digital solutions for some of the world's largest brands. Alongside his corporate endeavours, Joff is a sought-after Speaker and workshop facilitator.

In his spare time, Joff and his wife George are kept busy (in the right way) with their three young children. They live close to the Royal National Park in Sydney, Australia.

Acknowledgements

From Brad

To my wife, Ashlee. For your unwavering support every time I come to you and say 'I have an idea'. You stand by me going down the rabbit hole every time. Thank you.

From Joff

Firstly, thank you to my wife George, who has always been (and always will be) the better half. Thank you to my wonderful children Arthur, Louis and Eve for making me laugh every single day without fail.

Thank you to Andy Polaine for our decade-long (and counting) conversation about rubbish PowerPoint presentations, design and sourdough bread.

Finally, thank you to my beautiful Mum and my Dad, the best business mentor anyone could ever ask for.

Introduction

What/who is a Busy Idiot?

First, a confession. Joff's guilty pleasure is watching *Ramsay's Kitchen Nightmares.* He can happily waste an entire evening watching chef Gordon Ramsay become increasingly exasperated with restaurant owners before he finally gets his way by simplifying the menu and painting the walls white instead of crimson. Ramsay has a unique talent for insults, and in one episode he utters the words, which still resonate with Joff 13 years after the show aired:

'... you're a busy idiot.'

It was directed at a chef and it was anything but a compliment.

So what does it mean in the context of this book?

A Busy Idiot is like a hamster on a treadmill, running at breathtaking speed but going nowhere fast. They set up a meeting without an agenda and spend much of the meeting discussing what the agenda should be. So they set up another meeting, again with no agenda, and this goes on week after week. Busy Idiots are masters of multitasking; there's nothing they can't do ... provided it takes less than 30 minutes. They have no time to focus on bigger, more important strategic projects. Their phone is like a gun in a holster ready to be drawn the instant they feel it vibrate. They respond to emails too at lightning speed. Their emails often contain open-ended questions, which lead to more emails. They change their minds constantly; what was important yesterday is forgotten the next day. Everything has to be done *now*, everything is *urgent!*

In meetings, they nod along enthusiastically but they're not listening. In virtual meetings, they have several instant messaging conversations on the go. They love the pace and the dopamine kick from getting work done! Except work is never done. The busy idiot works longer and longer hours. Their calendar looks like a maniacal game of Tetris, with the sound on full blast. The business results don't follow and team attrition is high. Business leaders sometimes defend the busy idiot and point to their long hours and hard work, but the reality is that a busy idiot is just busy being busy.

Here, admittedly with more than a dash of hyperbole, is what a week in the life of a Busy Idiot might look like in a modern workplace. We sincerely hope this story doesn't feel too familiar to you.

Busy Idiot Jon

Jon works as a Customer Experience (CX) manager at a leading UK bank. It's his job to monitor customer feedback and sentiment and identify ways to improve the bank's net promoter score (NPS). His key performance indicator (KPI) is improving revenue growth by selling more home loans. Jon lives with his wife Sam, who also works fulltime, and their two young boys aged nine and eleven.

Jon starts Monday morning with no clear picture of what he's going to do or achieve. Instead, he dives into his inbox and works through the 50 emails he's received over the weekend. They're mostly internal, and it's lunchtime before he's answered them all. After lunch Jon dials into his series of diarised 1v1s with his team of four. The conversations are unstructured and informal. They're supposed to last 30 minutes but often go on longer. Jon does most of the talking, thinking out loud about some of the challenges the bank is facing. He rarely asks for his team members' ideas. At the end of each call he typically dishes out some half-baked actions. His team have learned to ignore these actions, as Jon usually forgets what he's asked them to do by the following week. Jon does this every Monday. In the evening, through dinner with his family, he sits at the end of the table scrolling his phone and answering emails.

On Tuesday, Jon prepares for the internal reporting call with his superiors that happens every Wednesday fortnight. He reviews all the NPS data and customer feedback and fills in a spreadsheet, a PowerPoint and an agenda for the call, which is attended by the Chief Financial Officer (CFO), Chief Operating Officer (COO) and his boss, the Chief Marketing Officer (CMO). Jon gets stressed about this meeting and spends the whole day crafting his narratives and making sure the presentation looks perfect. As he works through the report, he realises he needs the help of some of his team members and pings one of them on Slack, the bank's instant messaging platform. His direct report is working on a customer problem but he tells her to prioritise his request. It's super important for 'internal PR' that this report is right, he explains. He fiddles and frets over the report into the night, worried that his superiors might grill him on the decline in sales last month.

On Wednesday, after a rubbish night's sleep, Jon is already feeling the strain from a busy start to the week. He's scheduled a few internal catch ups with some peers to check how they're going. There's nothing specific to discuss. The meetings are mostly friendly chitchat and as the meetings near their end Jon suggests some potential collaboration areas, but nothing concrete. This gives him the opportunity to arrange follow-up meetings. Never end a meeting without setting up a follow-up meeting is one of Jon's mantras!

In the evening, Jon has his reporting call, shares the data and explains his strategic priorities for improving NPS. They're not really priorities as he lists off several ideas quickly. Some ideas seem contradictory. Jon suggests they need a laser focus on first-time buyers. Later, he suggests that they're not focusing enough on the property investment market, which is critical. His superiors struggle to follow his narrative. They spend most of their time questioning whether the data is right, as if the numbers will magically improve if they talk about them in detail. The meeting ends with a few stern motivational messages. The CFO tells Jon to buckle down and hit his numbers. His boss, the CMO, concludes with, yes and let us know how we can help. What that help might be is not specified. Jon is relieved to get through the call and hopes the numbers will improve by the time they meet again. It's 9 pm by the time the meeting ends and his two boys have already gone to bed. He heads downstairs to eat a plate of food wrapped in tin foil in front of the TV with Sam.

On Thursday, Jon sets up a meeting to play back the feedback from the previous night's meeting to his team. He hasn't had time to condense his thoughts, so it's an off-the-cuff hour's run-through of almost everything that was said. Jon ends the meeting by setting up a further meeting on Friday to 'brainstorm' how they might improve home loan sales. He also decides to join an internal virtual workshop on risk and resilience, even though this doesn't mean much to his role. While in this meeting, he flicks 50+ messages back and forth to his team on Slack. Two hours later he realises the workshop ended 30 minutes ago and he's the only one still dialled into the virtual meeting. On Thursday nights, Jon sometimes meets a friend for a game of squash, but he doesn't have the energy today and instead winds down with a few glasses of wine. He lets out a big sigh and tells himself, *Almost there!*

On Friday, Jon hosts a three-hour virtual brainstorm with his team. With no structure to the conversation, it quickly turns into an extended rant. The team share their frustrations regarding what they can't do because of red tape in the business and lack of capacity in the marketing and technology teams. Jon scribbles a few things on his notepad. At the end of the meeting he thanks the team. 'There's plenty of food for thought here,' he says. Jon rounds off the week by spending 90 minutes doing his timesheet. It takes him longer than usual as he needs to hunt down a code and get approval to register the time he spent in the internal risk workshop. Jon feels jaded after his week. When he gets home, he opens another bottle of wine and complains to Sam that he's been flat out. He forgets to ask her how her week has been. After dinner, he takes his glass of wine and laptop into his study and answers a few more emails. He closes his laptop at 9 pm, already dreading the emails that will rack up over the weekend...

Jon spent the week in a busy trap. His job is to drive customer NPS and ultimately revenue, yet he didn't interact with customers once, nor did he do anything directly for the bank's customers. Plus, on several occasions he distracted his team away from working with customers. This story is all too common in many corporations.

Here's the spoiler. You may think you're nothing like Jon. You may have picked up this book in the hope it will give you some sort of validation that your boss is a busy idiot (and he/she might well be), but in all likelihood you too are a busy idiot — hopefully not all the time, but at least some of the time.

We waste too many hours of our lives being busy idiots. Over the past two decades Joff has worked across the UK, the US and Australia for small and mid-size digital agencies with 25 to 50 employees and at some of the largest management and tech consultancies in the world with over 500 000 employees. Busywork has been a fixture to some degree across all these organisations and geographies.

In a 2013 YouGov survey of over 1000 Brits conducted by the late anthropologist David Graeber, 37 per cent of respondents felt they had 'a bullshit job' (15 per cent weren't sure). His definition of 'a bullshit job' was one that offers no value to the business or the person doing the job. Therefore, potentially as many as half of these British workers felt their job had no meaning. It's hard to see how things have improved over the past decade; the modern corporate workplace is a breeding ground for busy idiots, and western societies champion busyness.

Did we take a wrong turn?

Imagine working in an office in the 1950s. You'd likely have a typewriter and a rotary phone (with a switchboard to connect calls), and your storage device was a filing cabinet and a Rolodex. Office news would be posted on a bulletin board. Letters were the primary mode of business communication and could take a week or more to be delivered. Work was manual and slow. Most workers worked 40 hours a week and overtime was uncommon. Today we exchange correspondence in real time over email. We have instant messaging platforms, the internet and AI tools to give us information instantaneously. So why are we all so goddamn busy?

As the technology has evolved we've got busier. The technology has given rise to an always-on culture (sometimes an expectation) and workers are suffering. A 2022 survey by McKinsey Health of 15 000 workers across 15 countries found that a quarter of employees experienced burnout symptoms. Many surveys put the number much higher. Qualtrics found that 79 per cent of workers across 26 countries felt 'at or beyond workload capacity' at the height of the pandemic in 2020. The other epidemic that's not discussed is loneliness. In a Meta/Gallup study in October 2023 nearly one in four adults across the world reported feeling very or fairly lonely. Technology was supposed to make us more efficient and better connected, but we're still working at least 40 hours a week on average and we're lonelier than ever. Go figure.

Give me some good news ...

The good news is there's psychology and science behind why technology drives burnout and loneliness. By becoming aware of what happens to your brain when you spend your day pinging, swiping, texting and instant messaging, you can start to make adjustments and take back control. Sounds easy, right? Wrong! The tech industry utilises sophisticated persuasive design and artificial intelligence to actively hold your attention at work and at home. If you don't understand these techniques (at least on a base level), you are liable to become a 'lemming' — that's right, the 1991 hit game that took computer gaming by storm. Lemmings are green-haired, blue-robed little creatures that march in whatever direction their maker sees fit, even into oblivion (or off a cliff). Successful people avoid the busy traps of technology, and learn how to harvest technology and not let technology harvest them. We will show you how to do that in chapters 1 and 2 of this book.

What may feel out of your control is the way your organisation works, or more specifically the way your boss works. It can be torture to have a busy boss who flies by the seat of their pants and has ever-changing expectations and priorities. There are only two ways to solve this problem — meet it head-on or get out. Given that busywork is rife in most organisations, the latter is likely your plan B. It's better to hone a system to get control of your work and your boss. In chapter 3, we introduce some tried and tested techniques with supporting real-life anecdotes. Be prepared: these stories may feel like an episode of *The Office*, but they're all true.

Once you get a grip of your tech and your boss, you can start to make improvements to the way you work. Think of it as like adopting a healthy diet before you start hitting the gym. Joff's good friend and former colleague Dr Andy Polaine calls busywork the junk food of work. Like junk food, it can be addictive, but it's not good for you. And like any addiction, it needs constant discipline. Vicious cycles are much more seductive than virtuous ones. It takes discipline to ignore the lure of going into reactive, busy mode. Ultimately, your soul knows the difference between embracing meaningful work and cramming your day with as many micro-tasks and video calls as possible. In chapter 4, we'll cover what happens to your brain when you engage in busywork and why human connection is so important to fight loneliness and burnout.

So you've got control of your tech, you've got your boss in check, but you still can't do your best work. Most of us need to work in teams to achieve results. So how do you create a high-performing team? If you're not a manager or leader, you may think that's not your responsibility. And if you have a supportive and productive boss, maybe it's not entirely your burden to bear. If you have a busy boss, though, your alternative is to be the victim, let them set the tone for the team and spend most of your time griping with your colleagues. That time could be better spent introducing better ways for your teammates to meet, work and collaborate. The role of the leader isn't given or appointed; it's earned. You can be the one to get your team working smarter, and everyone will love you for it. Your organisation will recognise it too; the best way to get a promotion is to prove you can already do the job. In chapter 5, we'll introduce a practical toolkit for forming and leading productive and happy teams.

Finally, and most importantly, we shouldn't live to work. It's hard to be happy at home if you're stuck in a busy trap doing unproductive work all day. It leads to frustration that naturally bleeds into your private life. In chapter 6, we'll give you practical tips on how to make your home your castle to help you protect and cherish your family life. Ultimately, the aim of this book is to give you the gift of time. Time that can be better spent with those you love, doing the things you love. Time to disconnect from technology and connect with the people around you.

PART I
Manage your tech

CHAPTER 1

How did we get so goddamn busy?

Recently Brad was chatting with a mate, a very intelligent and successful medical doctor who is living the quintessential life: nice house and car, two kids and a dog. Actually they have a cat, but you get the idea.

Brad recalls talking to them about the family juggle and how they each manage the balance between work, relationships, self-care, the kids' school commitments, playdates, sport, medical appointments and everything else that goes with modern parenting. Throw in kids' gastro or brushes with COVID and you've got yourself a personal DEFCON 1 nightmare. He asked his mate, whose kids are a few years older than Brad's, how he manages all the competing priorities. There was silence for a while then a deep sigh. 'Who says I do?' They started mulling over past generations of parents and family and wondered if the lives in the 'family unit' (as we call it in psycho-babble) had always been under this much strain.

The answer? Yes … and no. Brad recalls growing up in the 1980s with two parents who worked extraordinarily hard and managed the juggle very well. They didn't appear to be running around like busy idiots. He had a clear picture in mind of his father coming home and launching into the usual chores — cooking dinner, cutting wood for the fire in winter, and no doubt arguing with his sons about chipping in. But when he left work, he left work. There was a clear delineation between work and home. Sure, in the event of some catastrophe he might get a call on the home phone, but there were no micro connections to work. No email, no group chats, no online shared workflow boards … When he was home, he was home.

We're not here to demonise technology. We recognise it's just one factor contributing to a new generation of unproductive busy idiots, but our work and research has convinced us that it is playing a major role and that its influence begins early. And we don't believe society has paid enough attention to the risks or side effects, especially over the past 10 years.

We challenge you to ask any primary school teacher how many kids aged five to seven in their class struggle with attention and focus. Then ask them whether this is different from 15 years ago. We understand a 'straw poll' isn't great science, but we think you'll find most of them report that historically it would be one or two children per class, whereas now it's more like four to six per class. The first smartphone arrived in 2007. Okay, so the academic researcher in Brad knows that correlation does not mean causation, but you can't tell us that's pure coincidence!

For us older humans (otherwise known as adults), we are all exposed increasingly in our personal lives to short-form videos (TikTok, Insta reels, YouTube shorts). While we complain that our teenagers can't stop watching short video clips, most of the time we're guilty of a fair dose of hypocrisy. Studies have shown that adults who frequently watch short-form video clips are prone to shorter attention span and are less accurate on tasks and less productive. You only have to see how short-form video clips are pushed in the mainstream media to know it 'works'. Have a look at any major newspaper online, and you'll soon find a section of short clips for quick consumption. What can we do about this? Don't worry, we have you covered. Chapter 2 will give you a roadmap.

In Brad's research lab 2000 Australian kids were surveyed in the largest study of its kind in the country. It found the average Aussie teen spends 9.5 hours a day on recreational screen use (phone, laptop, streaming, gaming, social media). This has been steadily increasing over the past decade.

We now have a generation of teenagers using screens and technology almost 10 hours a day outside of school. These teenagers will be the next crop of bright-eyed, ambitious workers running our global companies. Do they know how to maintain a healthy relationship with technology? All indications suggest they don't. Anyone at a mid-size to large organisation will tell you those staff in their twenties are a huge asset because of their tech-savvy skills. But for most of them their biggest asset is also their weakness. They don't know how to live with a Sustainable Tech Blueprint. And it's our fault, because we don't either, and you can't teach what you don't know.

Learn how to harvest tech with the Sustainable Tech Blueprint

Over the past five years we have rolled out technology at work and at home at breakneck speed. Most of this was with good intentions and productivity in mind, some of it by necessity given the circumstances we all found ourselves in around 2020. The world will never be the same. You can launch a business from your living room. You can work from a tropical beach in an exotic location many miles away from the major cities where we used to congregate. And perhaps best of all, many of us have adopted a hybrid model that has cut our commute significantly.

We found a panacea, right? Well, not so much. What we didn't plan on was the struggle for work/life balance, increased rates of burnout, lack of human connection and loneliness. And this is by no means an exhaustive list of the unintended consequences, but rather just a few of the more common ones.

We need to learn how to harvest technology, and not let technology harvest us.

This is precisely what we teach in workshops for organisations big and small. We call it the Sustainable Tech Blueprint. It has five steps (see figure 1.1):

1. **Sustainable awakening.** We are all in a kind of trance, allowing technology to creep into more and more areas of our lives and steal our attention. Before we can do anything, we need to *wake up* from this trance and open our minds to a different path.

2. **Sustainable knowing.** Knowledge is power. This step is all about the persuasive design that tech companies commonly use to attract and hold your attention.

3. **Sustainable audit.** This step is a deep dive into how you use technology. It asks that you hold up a mirror to see if your tech use is consistent with how you want to live. Don't worry, there are no reality-show mirrors in this step; we use an old-school tick-a-box questionnaire.

4. **Sustainable harvest.** How many of us have tried to rein in our tech use only to slip back into old habits? We use a series of 'harvest trees' (see pages 29–36) to find solutions that fit your goals.

5. **Sustainable grounding.** Grounding is all about getting back to living! By spending less time running around like busy idiots we gain control of our lives (as discussed in chapter 6).

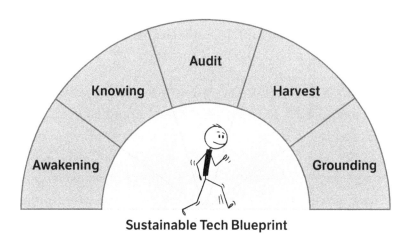

Figure 1.1: the five stages of the Sustainable Tech Blueprint

Sustainable knowing: learn the tenets of persuasive design

For any of you perceptive souls playing along at home you may have noticed we skipped *sustainable awakening*. The fact is everything you have read up to this point *is* your awakening. In buying this book you made a conscious decision to tackle the cycle of busyness. Awakening means being a willing participant in examining your own tech use and its impact. You made it this far, which means you are ready to tackle *sustainable knowing*, which delves into the world of *persuasive design*.

Persuasive design is the practice of applying a set of social and psychological principles to influence behaviour. It is commonly used in organisational management, e-commerce and population health interventions, often with positive net effect. It has also been used for the past 20 years or so in the tech industry to drive attention, traction, revenue and profits. Many of us are familiar with the concept and have a general idea of what it means, but don't understand the mechanics behind it. It's important to understand these mechanics if you plan to hack back the busyness trap.

A disclaimer here. There are a few books that cover some of these topics. You may have read them already. One thing we can guarantee is that our explanations are written in simple language and won't turn into a peer-reviewed thesis. You see, it's one thing to have an understanding of persuasive design, but it's quite another to be able to interpret how that impacts people at work and at home. Here's our quick-fire introduction to persuasive design.

Bartle's taxonomy: how your personality profile is used against you

Richard Bartle worked in AI before it was cool to do so. In the 1990s he coined a taxonomy that described four main 'player' profiles in any game. He suggested that we all fall into one of the following four profiles, and we derive our motivation for continuing to play the game from that core need being met:

1. *Achievers* focus on achieving the goals set in a game or app and attaining the status that comes from that.

2. *Killers* focus on winning at all costs and direct competition with peers.

3. *Socialites* focus on social interactions and networking within the game or platform.

4. *Explorers* focus on exploring and are motivated to discover new things.

This framing formed the basis of modern game design. It also heavily influences the design of the apps and social media you use at work and at home. If you are still scratching your head to think of a relevant example in your current tech blueprint, here's a subtle one most people can relate to.

You've no doubt been to a big work or industry conference or another huge event held at a major hotel or convention centre. Were you ever asked to download the conference app? It's for your convenience and will make the day run smoothly! Both are probably true, but it's also likely that the app is littered with persuasive design aimed at driving engagement, especially with the speakers and sponsors of the event who have typically paid money for their time in the spotlight.

A few years ago Brad attended a major conference on the Gold Coast in Queensland. A good friend and gaming addiction specialist, Dr Kim Le, was presenting a keynote on the final day. On day one it occurred to Brad that the conference app was gamified, with typical elements of game play like social competition, competitive rules and promoting a point system for completing certain tasks. Create a meeting hub connection (Socialites), 500 points. Visit an exhibitor (Explorers — after all, they are ensuring the financial viability of the conference), 1000 points. Add your photo in the profile settings (Socialites). And for the Killers (thankfully not in the literal sense) and Achievers, there was a live feed leaderboard!

Dr Le decided he would illustrate Bartle's taxonomy in his keynote and proceeded to use his power for evil, rising to the top of the leaderboard and explaining how he claimed the victory during his keynote. Being the only other person in the room with an in-depth understanding of persuasive design, Brad of course found this highly entertaining. The conference convenors, not so much. The prize was a free pass to the conference the following year. We don't think our good friend ever received that prize! Okay, so is Bartle's taxonomy of player profiles harmful to us as humans when used to drive engagement at a conference? Probably not. But as we noted at the start of this chapter, knowledge is power, so think about how your user (player) data and profile inform how technology targets you, persuading you to stay engaged. Your attention is the commodity.

Flow: how you lose track of time

Flow refers to the idea that all technology and app design is based on continuing to increase the level of difficulty for the user while at the same time increasing the level of skill required to operate that app or program. This magical middle ground between the two is referred to as 'Flow' and is associated with the distortion of time. Quite literally, we spend more time in that world than we consciously intend.

To ensure we're not demonising the modern workplace, let's use an example with more personal responsibility attached. Almost a decade ago Brad was working at a university in the Sydney CBD. Every morning he would join the masses on the train commute.

A side note: Next time you are on public transport put your phone away for just 10 minutes and count how many people you can see who have done the same. It won't be many. In our observations it's usually under 10 per cent. And of those who don't have their phone in their hand (like Brad, Joff reads his Kindle!), they are usually listening to music but are at least observing the world around them.

Back to Brad's train commute. Every morning he would catch the train from his inner-west home to the CBD. There was usually a corporate worker in the same carriage (three rows up) who was completely obsessed with the mobile app game 'Candy Crush Saga'. For those of you who are not familiar, the object of the game is to line up the fruits or candies so they magically disappear, triggering lights, sounds and points flashing. Each level requires more skill than the last, which makes it like a game of Flow. And every morning our poor friend from three rows up would lose track of her surroundings and often miss her stop. It became a running evening debrief between Brad and his wife, Ashlee.

Ashlee: 'Did candy crush lady make her stop today?'

Brad: 'No, but she was so close this time. She made it up the stairs right as the doors closed on her. Do you think I should tap her on the shoulder tomorrow when it's her stop?'

Ashlee: 'Hmm… I know you're trying to be helpful, but that would be weird.'

So the game of closing train doors continued.

Brad still thinks about that lady, and wonders if her innocent obsession with Candy Crush Saga that stole her attention and time ever impacted her life in other ways? At home? At work? Okay, it's weird, but this is the stuff that keeps Brad up at night.

Dopamine: how tech biohacks your neurochemicals

We could write a whole book on this but we won't, because you'd likely fall asleep while Brad geeked out on the neurochemical jargon. So let's keep it simple.

Dopamine is a feel-good chemical. You can find it in most things humans enjoy: chocolate, drugs, sex… Tech platforms are incredibly good at delivering dopamine. Especially when the apps or platforms driving our use are social in nature. Dopamine delivery can be measured by various scans including a functional MRI (fMRI), which will show which areas of the brain light up in response to different stimuli. Tech platforms can achieve this by using what was once known in the industry as 'dopamine labs' to test design features and how well they deliver dopamine. For example, TV streaming platforms will test multiple combinations of colours, brightness and sounds to optimise dopamine delivery to the user.

In 2014, a Scandinavian research lab ran an fMRI study in which they made what we believe is one of the most important discoveries in the field of screen and technology addiction. They discovered that the levels of dopamine in 'offline' games, although significant, were not as high as the levels of dopamine when playing online.

What does that mean? When you make something more social, it delivers a bigger dopamine hit. Even if you never meet these people in the real world! The more phone data and WiFi we enable in our work and home lives, the more we seek that dopamine.

Now, here is a cool (and by cool we mean incredibly scary) note. The dopamine hit we get from our technology devices is very small and constant. It does not crescendo. It is what's known as anticipatory dopamine. We never get the full hit, just the anticipation high. This results in a constant loop of craving technology without ever feeling satisfied.

The near-miss effect: falling just short, but you still get a dopamine hit

This effect, also known as the 'fun/failure effect', occurs when your tech sets you a task and you come so close to achieving it but you fall just short. You keep trying despite not getting there, and seldom become discouraged!

Pop quiz: This element of persuasive design has its origins in which industry?

That's right, gambling. This is the basis of most poker (slot) machines. You can lose on a given spin but the machine goes off with lights, sounds, fireworks, as if you've won! You have a net loss in financial terms, but you are encouraged to spin again.

Business apps use this design method too. Think of the business networking social media or platforms we commonly use. The constant feedback around how much of your profile or goal you have completed (usually given in a percentage bar) and notifications and prompts to complete the task. Why are they so detail oriented about this? Engagement. Your time *is* the commodity in advertising and other revenue streams.

The hyperpersonal effect: how online content is more powerful than the real world

This effect refers to how the emotional power and cognitive salience of anything said online can be more powerful than the same thing said in person. Put simply, a comment (good or bad) about you personally or your work performance made in an online chat group, workflow platform or email chain can have far greater impact than if it was said around the office. It is part of the reason we are driven to use the tech our workplace affords us.

Social comparison theory: how tech undermines our self-worth

This is linked to the hyperpersonal effect, but distinguished by the need or drive to compare our failures and successes with those of others we see online. Constantly comparing ourselves can drive busy idiot behaviours in an endless loop and throw us off what we set out to achieve for that hour, morning or day.

The Work From Home (WFH) and hybrid work movements were not the starting bell for Social Comparison Theory, but they sure do afford us an abundance of examples. We all have a friend or work colleague who always seems incredibly switched on at virtual meetings — well dressed and alert, with an array of serious-looking books behind them. Or perhaps the meeting platform has provided them with impressive props that include a mahogany desk and a 16th-floor city view. Clearly one of life's winners.

The truth is often far from what is portrayed. In reality, beyond this carefully contrived set the rest of the house looks like a bomb hit it, and the kids are drawing on the walls or one step short of sibling assault. Welcome to social comparison theory.

We compare ourselves to the perfectly manicured version we see online, rather than the reality.

Brad has a confession. He too is guilty of playing to the social comparison theory. A few years ago he was doing a live TV cross with famed Australian news anchor Michael Usher. The world saw his perfectly staged bookshelves, his suit jacket and sharp haircut, not his shorts and Ugg boots just out of camera shot. They didn't see his toddler son crash through the baby gate he had installed (yep, definitely not a handyman) and fall face first down a flight of stairs during the broadcast. It crossed his mind that he could be the next viral meme of a live TV interview with a screaming child crashing the party. But those who watched the nightly news from home, they saw only another expert preaching from the comfort of his perfect home. Brad recently told Michael Usher that story when they worked together on another project. He had no idea of the chaos that unfolded at the Marshall house that day. Definitely felt like a busy idiot moment.

The Zeigarnik effect: why we can't resist the 'pings'

This phenomenon refers to our tendency to recall uncompleted tasks better than tasks we have completed. Extending this into social psychology, it is the desire to seek out a logical conclusion to social interactions. Just think on that one for a moment. We need to know what happens in any social interaction. It's how we are wired as humans. We crave it.

How do tech companies play on the Zeigarnik effect? It's another one that we will try to abbreviate with a few examples, but you will see it everywhere your life intersects technology.

A few years ago most software updates for smartphones and messaging platforms on computers and tablets rolled out amazing advancements. You could now see who had read your message and what time they received it, which risks drawing you into overdrive paranoia: *Mike read that message, so what's his problem? Why hasn't he responded to my proposal? Maybe he doesn't like it. Is this going to affect my performance review next week?*

That is the Zeigarnik effect in action. The constant need to understand the social outcome in any given situation. And it doesn't just happen at work. Think about how many messaging apps we get stuck reading when we are supposed to be living life. How many times have Joff and Brad disappeared down a rabbit hole, reading messages from our Fantasy Premier League chat group (yes, we're both football tragics) when we should be doing focused work or watching our kids' sport?

Understand persuasive design's endgame

Charlie Munger was the vice-chairman of Berkshire Hathaway, Warren Buffett's right-hand man and the architect of the investment firm's modern philosophy. Charlie once said, 'Show me the incentive and I'll show you the outcome.'

AI/social media experts and industry whistle-blowers Tristan Harris and Aza Raskin refer to this technology as 'first generation AI'. We'll touch on 'second generation AI' later in the book.

The endgame is this: *attention + focus = revenue*. Plain and simple. We don't doubt many tech companies start with noble intentions to improve our lives, but you'd be hard pressed to find one that doesn't employ persuasive design to turn you into a busy idiot. Persuasive design in technology prevents you from working efficiently during the working day. This leads to long hours, the blurring of work/life balance and an overwhelming feeling of busyness.

How did we get so goddamn busy?

....

1. **The Sustainable Tech Blueprint**

   - *Awakening:* Tune in and reflect on your tech use at work and at home.

   - *Knowing:* Understand the power of persuasive design.

   - *Auditing:* Evaluate whether your tech use is consistent with how you want to live.

   - *Harvesting:* Use decision-making trees to wrestle your tech back into line with your goals.

   - *Grounding:* Get back to spending time on meaningful and enriching activities.

 Top tip: Learn how to harvest technology, rather than letting technology harvest you!

2. **Persuasive design**

   - Bartle's taxonomy teaches us about player profiles and what drives us to consume tech.

- Flow is a design feature used by apps and tech to keep the user engaged, which often induces a sense of time lost.

- The near-miss effect is a design feature in which the achievement or goal is slightly out of reach, yet it still delivers a dopamine hit to the user.

- Dopamine is a feel-good neurochemical released by tech.

- The hyperpersonal effect recognises the greater emotional power and 'pull' of online rather than offline connection.

- Social comparison theory refers to the human compulsion to compare our successes and failures with those we see online.

- The Zeigarnik effect acknowledges that we crave a logical conclusion or outcome to social interactions.

 Top tip: Think about how your tech targets and commodifies you, persuading you to stay engaged.

CHAPTER 2

How to stop bouncing around like a Busy Idiot

We have walked through the Sustainable Tech Blueprint and how persuasive design (sustainable knowing) is a busy trap. Now we'll turn our attention to concrete strategies. This chapter introduces a questionnaire and decision-making tools that focus on the changes you need to make as an individual to bring your tech use back in line with your goals and values. Chapters 3 and 5 will look at how to deal with a busy boss and how to form productive teams at work.

Remember our trip through nineties pop culture royalty from the start of this book and avoid the busy lemming traps of technology and learn how to harvest technology rather than letting technology harvest them. So we have put off the uncomfortable look in the mirror for long enough. It's time to talk about a sustainable audit.

Audit your tech use

A sustainable audit is exactly what it suggests. We are going to audit our tech use to determine whether it's in line with what *you* think is a happy and healthy tech blueprint. There's no magic number, but by now you should have at least a general idea of how you want to harvest technology.

Answer the questions posed on the next page honestly, based on your past few months' experience.

After you've braved the sustainable audit! Calculate your total score and claim your badge.

How tech fit are you?

	1 point	2 points	3 points	4 points	Score
I find myself checking my phone while eating a meal?	Never	Once a week	Most days	Multiple times a day	
My partner/family/friends complain about my being glued to a device or screen?	Never	Rarely	Often	Always	
If I try, I can reduce the time I spend on my phone for a while, but I end up using it as much or even more than before.	Never	Rarely	Often	Always	
I find myself sending/ checking work emails outside of work hours.	Never	Once a week	Once a day	Multiple times a day	
I use my phone as a way of changing my mood (e.g. to get a buzz, reduce stress or escape).	Never	Rarely	Often	Always	
While spending time with family or friends I mindlessly check my phone.	Never	Rarely	Often	Always	
I find myself checking my phone while in virtual/ physical meetings.	Never	Rarely	Often	Always	
In virtual meetings I'll often multitask and scroll or read/answer emails.	Never	Rarely	Often	Always	
Total score					

Score	Badge
25–32	Tech busy idiot
20–24	Tech busy idiot candidate
15–19	Tech busy idiot tendencies
8–14	You're Bear Grylls, a proper boy scout. Do you even own a phone?

Harvest tech — some software solutions

In our experience, many people are at least vaguely aware of the dangers of a heavy tech blueprint. So why is it that they struggle to implement real-world change that sticks? That, my friends, is the secret sauce. It's easy for an 'expert' to grandstand online or in the media about how we need to cut back. It's easy for academics and researchers to tell us to put the phone down. But how do we actually achieve that? The tech industry has already solved this problem. Smartphone manufacturers have all sorts of in-built features including 'Focus' mode, a 'do not disturb' setting, screentime tracking — the list goes on. So why do these features fall short in helping us to say no to our phone? Let's for a moment put aside the fact that the technology industry is an ecosystem that, on a macro level, benefits from our *constant* attention. At the risk of sounding cynical and jaded, their profits rely on these features being ineffective, or our not utilising them. But let's let that one go through to the keeper and assume they have noble intentions towards you, the human being using their device.

Focus (Apple) or Focus Time (Google)

As a concept, it sounds incredible. Sign us up! We dedicated a full hour recently to tackling this one to provide us with some more focused time when working on our research. But it soon hit us. Has *anyone* successfully used these features on their phone? We are iPhone users and would describe ourselves as 'mid- to high-level' tech savvy. But wow, are they complicated to set up, navigate and use! Different profiles, home screens, backgrounds, times, stop some people from calling or allow others to call, but then can't stop them from texting ... Phew! Why is it this hard?

On Brad's phone, the end result was a home screen map of the world (which to be fair looked pretty cool) that showed nothing but the local time and a polite reminder that it was 10.19 pm in Cupertino … Where the heck is Cupertino? And how did that get onto his Focus home screen? While we have not road-tested the Focus time software for other smartphones, we get real-world feedback every time we work with an organisation. And, judging by the lack of uptake, it appears the Android software leads to similar outcomes.

Do not disturb features don't save you from yourself

So this feature is slightly more friendly to navigate. For our fellow iPhone people, you find it under the same Focus menu, and there is far less flexibility to customise it, which is strangely liberating. But we have two main criticisms.

First, you can stop certain groups from calling, but allow them to text. For example, if Brad doesn't want a call from his dear old father but would like him to be able to send a text in an emergency (or the other way around depending on how your family communicates), you can't do that in this setting. The result? Massive FOMO. Or, in technical language, the Zeigarnik effect plays on your neurological need for social conclusion.

Second, you can stop notifications from certain apps in the DND feature, but this doesn't block you from mindlessly navigating the home screen to open that app. The result? One minute Brad is crunching complicated data and running regression analysis, the next he has opened the FotMob app for the latest Premier League news … Sound familiar?

Screentime: the lock doesn't work if you have the key

Most of you will be familiar with Screentime: you can set a time limit on individual apps; it tracks your usage and shuts it down when you hit your predefined limit. That's a great concept. It's like someone telling you to go on a health kick and only eat fruit and vegetables. You commit to it for a few days, but at the first sign of stress at work or home it's out the window. Screentime can be easily circumvented using the passcode. Most adults will find themselves entering the passcode multiple times, and their original commitment to a sustainable tech blueprint is GONE!

Some consider Brad an expert in the field of the psychology and neuroscience of screens and gaming. So let's share his secret: Ashlee has the passcode for his screentime. Really, that's the truth. He has Screentime on his phone, mostly to limit his use of social media. And as a pre-commitment to prevent the above-mentioned cycle, he asked Ashlee to set the passcode. The temptation to ask her for more time on social media is outweighed by his disappointment in himself for breaking that commitment.

Greyscale

We were alerted to this feature by a helpful workshop participant who told us they had found it helpful. This feature basically drains the colour from your screen, making it less appealing and your phone less shiny and distracting. For those on IOS, see if you can find it for yourself, just intuitively. Bet you can't! Why would they make it easy to find? That would mean you might use it! You can turn your screen greyscale in *five* steps:

1. Settings
2. Accessibility *(obvious next step, right?)*
3. Display and text *(ohh yeah, very logical next step)*
4. Colour filters
5. Greyscale.

Even if you manage to navigate your way to turning this function on, you're unlikely to keep it on. The first time you need to see a document or picture in colour you go back to the original colour. Then, when considering switching back to grey, you need to fumble your way through the five steps again. Unlikely.

I'm just annoyed—tell me what to do!

Most professionals we speak to privately admit they've tried these features and just couldn't stick it out. It often generates anger, resentment and frustration. 'Is there something wrong with me? Because my phone has all these tools that are supposed to help me, but they just don't!' While some of the tools and features tech companies roll out are helpful, please understand that none of them are perfect, even for us. If you have a colleague or family member who boasts about their amazing self-control with their phone, we strongly suggest they are one of the following:

1. an amazing human being (the rare exception)

2. lying to make themselves look good

3. delusional.

Oh, and if anyone knows where Cupertino is please DM Brad.

Consider hardware solutions to reduce your tech addiction

Think of software solutions (like the ones for your phone just described) as your first line of defence. They are nice, but they're full of loopholes and unlikely to work in isolation. Hardware solutions are akin to a sledgehammer solution. They can be inconvenient at times, but overall they're more effective at reducing our screen time and distraction.

A few years ago, Brad took his family to Sea World on the Gold Coast. Incredible place. Everything one would expect from an amusement park next to a resort on a picturesque beach. The week before he left he was feeling anxious. He had a picture in mind of how memorable these sorts of family trips are for kids. He has vivid memories of going to Disneyland in Florida USA at around the same age and being suitably frightened of Goofy. Like many of us, he didn't want to be a Busy Idiot, responding to work or social pings on his phone while walking around the theme park. He desperately didn't want his kids to have that memory of their holiday. He had some software solutions in place — mainly Screentime on social media — but didn't want to be tempted by work emails or doomscrolling the news. It was time for a hardware solution. Brad bought an Apple watch. More technology? That's crazy! Let us explain.

He deleted everything but the basics from the Apple watch. Music, run tracker app, messages, phone calls (he had it linked to his phone plan) and a few apps that Apple annoyingly makes you keep even if you don't want them. But no emails. No messenger apps. No social media.

Some people love the fitness and health tracking goals on smartwatches. We get it, theoretically it takes the guesswork out of how active you are, how many steps you need, your exercise and standing goals for the day. If that's your thing, go for it. But we find these health goals intrusive, so we delete them or turn off the notifications. If we need an app or algorithm to gamify health and fitness via Pavlovian vibrations to our wrist, then we reckon we have bigger problems and need to take a long hard look at our lifestyle choices.

By way of pre-commitment, Brad left his smartphone in the hotel room. The result was pure relaxation and freedom, though he did draw some odd looks while trying to coordinate a meetup with Ashlee via voice-activated text messages on his watch, looking like a lost James Bond wannabe. It was probably the most 'present' he had been with his family in years, and he continues to replicate that combination for family activities most weekends. When his kids are down at the local beach surf life-saving club training on a Sunday morning, you'll find him rocking a smartwatch and no phone. It's just one example of what we call a hardware solution. You're shifting to hardware devices that may be less functional but ensure less distraction.

A smartwatch is not the only answer here. Perhaps you don't like wearing a watch or don't want the added expense. As an antidote to smartphones, dumb phones are becoming increasingly popular again. A dumb phone is like the mobile phone we had as kids: it made calls and sent texts and its battery lasted for days! No apps, no games (well, Snake came later on the Nokia 6110, but hey …) and no distractions. Consider using a dumb phone on weekends to better disconnect from work. The third alternative of course is to abandon tech altogether! Sounds unthinkable, we know, but it was the norm through our early childhood. Put a credit card or some cash in your pocket and enjoy time with your family.

If you ask cybersecurity experts, they will tell you they use 'layers' of security to ensure information is kept safe. Harvest trees are like layers of security (hardware and software) you can implement.

Use harvest trees to find what works best for you

Let's take the guesswork out of the sustainable harvest. The following pages present a series of harvest trees that will help you run through the common software and hardware solutions you might consider for various technologies. Find the ones that best resonate with you. Happy harvesting.

Sustainable audit and *harvest* are not a one-time, set-and-forget deal. Technology continues to change rapidly, so we have to keep learning how to harvest it. We recommend auditing your tech at least once a year, followed by the harvest trees.

Emails to go

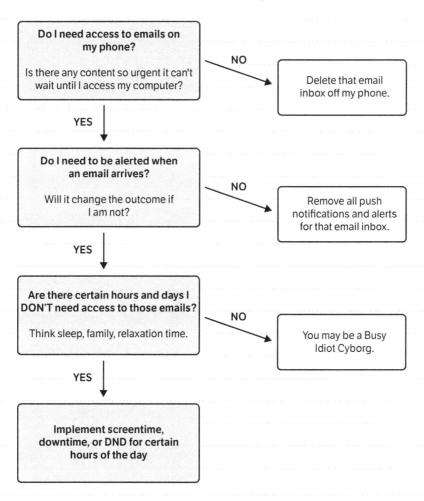

Do I need access to emails on my phone?

Is there any content so urgent it can't wait until I access my computer?

NO → Delete that email inbox off my phone.

YES ↓

Do I need to be alerted when an email arrives?

Will it change the outcome if I am not?

NO → Remove all push notifications and alerts for that email inbox.

YES ↓

Are there certain hours and days I DON'T need access to those emails?

Think sleep, family, relaxation time.

NO → You may be a Busy Idiot Cyborg.

YES ↓

Implement screentime, downtime, or DND for certain hours of the day

Get out of your inbox

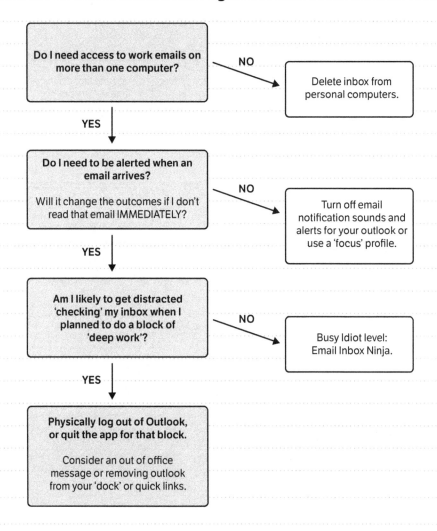

Do I need access to work emails on more than one computer?

NO → Delete inbox from personal computers.

YES ↓

Do I need to be alerted when an email arrives?

Will it change the outcomes if I don't read that email IMMEDIATELY?

NO → Turn off email notification sounds and alerts for your outlook or use a 'focus' profile.

YES ↓

Am I likely to get distracted 'checking' my inbox when I planned to do a block of 'deep work'?

NO → Busy Idiot level: Email Inbox Ninja.

YES ↓

Physically log out of Outlook, or quit the app for that block.

Consider an out of office message or removing outlook from your 'dock' or quick links.

Screen your screen time

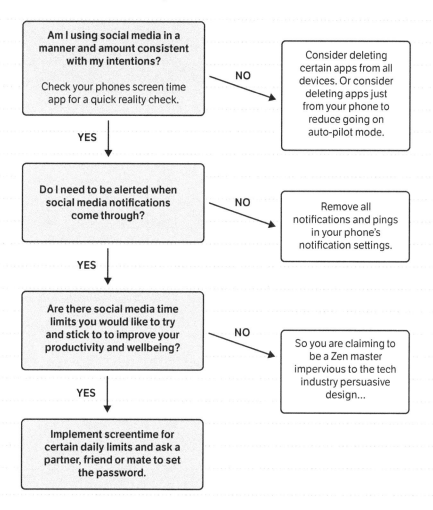

Am I using social media in a manner and amount consistent with my intentions?

Check your phones screen time app for a quick reality check.

NO → Consider deleting certain apps from all devices. Or consider deleting apps just from your phone to reduce going on auto-pilot mode.

YES ↓

Do I need to be alerted when social media notifications come through?

NO → Remove all notifications and pings in your phone's notification settings.

YES ↓

Are there social media time limits you would like to try and stick to to improve your productivity and wellbeing?

NO → So you are claiming to be a Zen master impervious to the tech industry persuasive design...

YES ↓

Implement screentime for certain daily limits and ask a partner, friend or mate to set the password.

The temple of doom(scrolling)

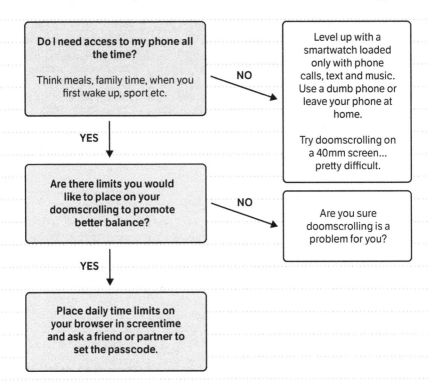

Do I need access to my phone all the time?

Think meals, family time, when you first wake up, sport etc.

NO → Level up with a smartwatch loaded only with phone calls, text and music. Use a dumb phone or leave your phone at home.

Try doomscrolling on a 40mm screen... pretty difficult.

YES ↓

Are there limits you would like to place on your doomscrolling to promote better balance?

NO → Are you sure doomscrolling is a problem for you?

YES ↓

Place daily time limits on your browser in screentime and ask a friend or partner to set the passcode.

Get the message

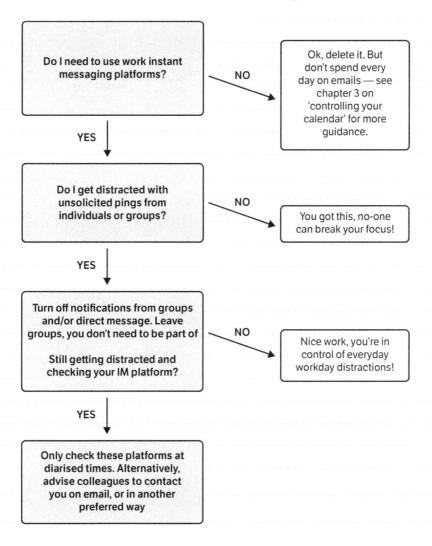

Do I need to use work instant messaging platforms?

NO → Ok, delete it. But don't spend every day on emails — see chapter 3 on 'controlling your calendar' for more guidance.

YES ↓

Do I get distracted with unsolicited pings from individuals or groups?

NO → You got this, no-one can break your focus!

YES ↓

Turn off notifications from groups and/or direct message. Leave groups, you don't need to be part of

Still getting distracted and checking your IM platform?

NO → Nice work, you're in control of everyday workday distractions!

YES ↓

Only check these platforms at diarised times. Alternatively, advise colleagues to contact you on email, or in another preferred way

Escape the messenger apps

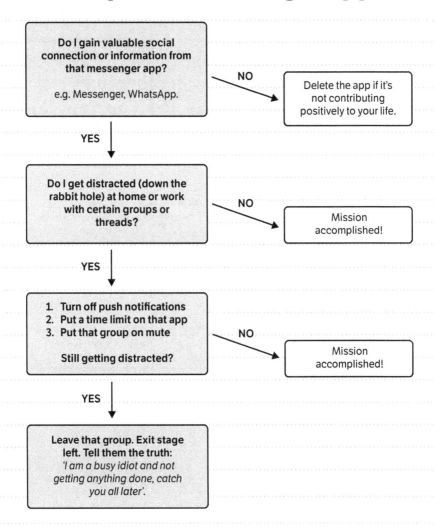

Do I gain valuable social connection or information from that messenger app?

e.g. Messenger, WhatsApp.

NO → Delete the app if it's not contributing positively to your life.

YES ↓

Do I get distracted (down the rabbit hole) at home or work with certain groups or threads?

NO → Mission accomplished!

YES ↓

1. Turn off push notifications
2. Put a time limit on that app
3. Put that group on mute

Still getting distracted?

NO → Mission accomplished!

YES ↓

Leave that group. Exit stage left. Tell them the truth: *'I am a busy idiot and not getting anything done, catch you all later'.*

Keeping watch

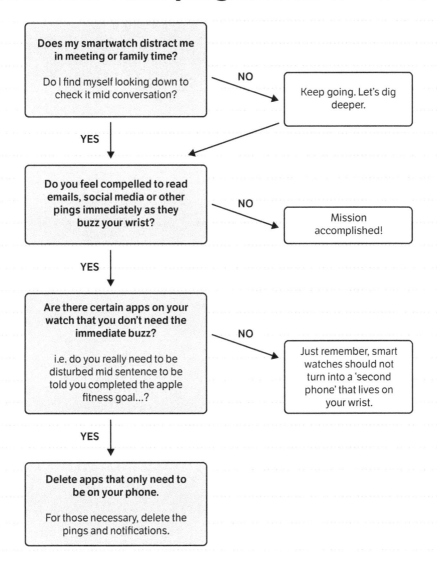

Does my smartwatch distract me in meeting or family time?

Do I find myself looking down to check it mid conversation?

NO → Keep going. Let's dig deeper.

YES ↓

Do you feel compelled to read emails, social media or other pings immediately as they buzz your wrist?

NO → Mission accomplished!

YES ↓

Are there certain apps on your watch that you don't need the immediate buzz?

i.e. do you really need to be disturbed mid sentence to be told you completed the apple fitness goal...?

NO → Just remember, smart watches should not turn into a 'second phone' that lives on your wrist.

YES ↓

Delete apps that only need to be on your phone.

For those necessary, delete the pings and notifications.

Stop the stream

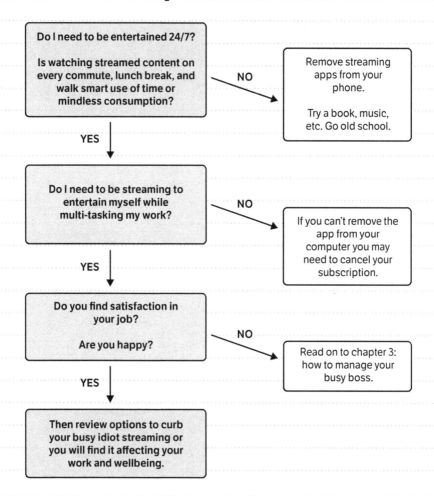

Do I need to be entertained 24/7?

Is watching streamed content on every commute, lunch break, and walk smart use of time or mindless consumption?

NO → Remove streaming apps from your phone.

Try a book, music, etc. Go old school.

YES ↓

Do I need to be streaming to entertain myself while multi-tasking my work?

NO → If you can't remove the app from your computer you may need to cancel your subscription.

YES ↓

Do you find satisfaction in your job?

Are you happy?

NO → Read on to chapter 3: how to manage your busy boss.

YES ↓

Then review options to curb your busy idiot streaming or you will find it affecting your work and wellbeing.

How to stop bouncing around like a Busy Idiot

Avoid the busy idiot technology traps.

1. **Sustainable audit**

   - There's no magic number for our sustainable audit questionnaire.

   - It's all about reflecting on the relationship you want with technology, and whether it results in a net gain or net loss in your life.

 Top tip: Audit your tech use at least once a year.

2. **Sustainable harvest**

   - Many of us have identified that we are unhappy with at least some of the impact technology has on our lives.

   - Taking charge can be hard. As any good cybersecurity expert will tell you, you need a multi-layered defence.

   - Harvest trees take the guesswork out of it. After every audit, check in on the harvest trees that apply to you.

 Top tip: Harvest technology sustainably — it's the new frontier.

PART II
Manage your work and family life

CHAPTER 3

How to manage your busy boss

When someone resigns they tell their boss they're leaving the company. They might post on LinkedIn: 'Today, after five great years, I've decided to leave company x. Excited about my next chapter!' The truth is, in most cases people don't leave the company, they leave their boss. Management institute / Gallup, interviewed 20 000 students and 20 000 managers globally and found that managers accounted for at least 70 per cent of the variance in employee engagement scores across business units. In large corporations, it's not uncommon for some to thrive while others of equal ability struggle. When it comes to your workplace satisfaction and success, a lot can depend on your reporting line. If you have a busy boss, that's tough luck. Busy bosses set sail at a rate of knots but they don't know where they're heading and will change direction with the wind. How can you get ahead successfully if your captain is lost at sea? This chapter will introduce some practical tips on how to navigate these treacherous waters. Sorry, enough of the nautical metaphors ... for now.

Natalie and her busy boss

Natalie breezed through university, picking up a first-class honours degree in Economics from a top London business school. As described by her friends, Natalie is confident, outgoing and headstrong. On graduation her future looked very bright, and after interviewing at several top firms in the FTSE 100, she decided the fast-paced world of management consulting would best suit her skills, ambitions and temperament. She joined one of the 'big four' as a management consulting analyst, specialising in digital transformation. She got off to a great start. After completing her induction and training, she worked on a five-month project where, as part of a team of four, she helped redesign an insurance claims process. It might not sound exciting but she loved the camaraderie in the team and took satisfaction from seeing a tedious paper-based claims process re-emerge in a slick, easy-to-use digital format. Natalie's job on the project was to document requirements for the digital tool. She got great feedback from the Project Lead and eagerly awaited her next assignment.

Time on the bench ...

But following the completion of the project there was no immediate client work for Natalie and she found herself 'on the bench'. Being 'benched' was a new experience for Natalie. She turned up to the office every day, but then didn't know what to do. Normally confident and outgoing, she kept her head down, worried that her superiors might think she was malingering. She found some online training that kept her busy for an hour a day, but otherwise found herself moving her mouse around aimlessly, feeling increasingly anxious and dejected.

Fortunately for Natalie, this experience lasted only a week, as she was pulled into a bid team to work on a government tender. It was an open tender (which meant any organisation could submit) from the Department of Justice to create a new online tool to assist citizens summoned for jury duty. The bid team was small — Natalie, a consultant named Jess (who was a level above her in seniority) and Gary, a director (several levels above her) overseeing the response. Gary called a briefing meeting to explain the project. He explained that the firm didn't have any relationships at the Department of Justice and that the opportunity had come out of the blue. The firm had limited experience in the Department of Justice's preferred technology platform for the jury duty portal. Gary described their bid as a 'moonshot' but added it was worth competing for, as 'stranger things have happened'. Plus, this would help him boost his sales pipeline numbers for his next call.

Government tenders aren't much fun. In order to make them as fair as possible, government departments ask for considerable detail (which makes it hard for small firms to compete, but that's a topic for another day). For this bid, Natalie and Jess were tasked with filling in a document with 25 questions about the firm's organisational and financial information, a document with 50 technical questions relating to the Department's preferred technology platform, a comprehensive proposal outlining their point of view on the challenge, project approach, deliverables and experience. They also had to provide a document that included CVs of the proposed team members, plus a detailed pricing Excel sheet. Alongside this, the Department's draft Master Services Agreement (a lengthy legal document that documents general terms and conditions between parties for future service engagements) had to be sent for legal review. Finally, all internal processes had to be followed for pricing and document quality assurance. Gary instructed Natalie and Jess to work fulltime on the project for the next two weeks. He would set up regular daily check-ins and help where he could; however, he made it clear that they'd need to do the heavy lifting as he had more important things to work on.

Jess, four years into life at the firm, spoke up first. She told Gary she would really love to work on the tender but unfortunately she had prior commitments. Jess explained how she had already promised a partner in the firm that she would help with an exciting bid to win a new airline client. She thought she might be able to juggle both but would only be able to attend the stand-ups sporadically and commit 50 per cent of her time. Gary said that was fine and told Natalie she would have to put in the 'hard yards' to make up the difference.

A confrontation ...

Natalie's blood was boiling. She felt like she was being told to work for two full weeks on a bid they had no chance of winning, with little or no help. The exchange with Gary did not go well:

Natalie: 'Gary, why are we doing this? It feels like a complete waste of time!'

Gary: 'I don't feel like that. You never know, we might win. And even if we don't, it might get us some traction with the Department of Justice.'

Natalie: 'Rather than doing all this work for two weeks, why don't you just ask to meet with the Director at the Department so we're better positioned next time?'

Gary: 'With respect, I don't need advice on how to do my job. When I was an analyst I had to do this stuff — it's good learning experience.'

Natalie: 'I don't see what I'd be learning other than how to submit a losing response.'

Gary: 'What else are you gonna do? You're on the bench. You may as well do this. I'll give you a template that you can work on, but we're bidding so let's crack on.'

Natalie put her head down and for the next two weeks struggled through the tender response the firm had no right to win. She worked 14-hour days tracking down case studies and content for the proposal. The firm submitted the proposal an hour before the deadline. Two weeks later they received a generic, automated response from the Department of Justice: 'Thank you for your response to our tender to redesign the jury duty experience for citizens. Unfortunately, on this occasion you have been unsuccessful. You may request a time to seek additional feedback.'

After two weeks of intense busywork Natalie felt burnt out, anxious and demoralised. To make matters worse, her reputation within the firm had also taken a hit. Gary shared to several Partners within the firm that she's difficult to work with and has a bad attitude. Natalie decided to leave the firm a few months later, feeling her chances of progression were limited.

What went wrong?

Joff has seen this scenario play out countless times during his 20 years' working in large corporations. You might think Gary was a jerk and that he was the problem (and you'd be partly right), but he'd had to do the same sort of work when he was coming up through the ranks. Busywork is an endemic part of corporate life that everyone must embrace at some stage. Working on a pointless tender response was a rite of passage. Plus, it would make Gary (as one of Natalie's superiors) look bad if he couldn't find something for her to do. The tender ticked the boxes from his perspective. He got to put a number in the pipeline, there was a (very slim) chance they might win and he didn't actually have to do the work. He could rationalise it as a learning experience for Natalie. The issue is that busywork like this is incredibly stressful; working hard on something that has no end goal is a form of spiritual torture.

So what could Natalie have done differently? The remainder of this chapter outlines seven practical techniques to manage your busy boss and take control of your career.

Control your calendar

There's no weapon more powerful for your defence against busywork and your busy boss than your calendar. It's your knight in shining armour. The defender of your time. Time is the most important resource in the whole world. Without time you have nothing. (Sorry for the hyperbole, but we hope you get the message.) First things first. Don't let your calendar control you through the dopamine the pings deliver via notifications.

If you need a refresh on the 'tech hacks' to control your calendar, revisit chapter 1. Your calendar (for now) doesn't proactively help you; you have to help your calendar to help you.

In the near future your calendar will use artificial intelligence to learn your patterns and help defend against time thieves, busywork and unnecessary stressful encounters. For now, it's on you. And you'll have to learn the good habits we're about to outline to train your new AI-assisted calendar. Otherwise, your new AI friend might propel you into more busyness under the impression that's what you want (more on this later in chapter 5).

Fail to plan, plan to be busy

If you walk into your working week like Natalie did with no idea what to expect, you risk spending the week unfocused and feeling lost, or worse you'll get suckered into a busy trap. There may be occasions, as in Natalie's case, when you'll have to commit to work you don't really want to do. However, your diary (plus the other tips outlined in this chapter) can help ensure this isn't the norm.

Firstly, never start the working week without an understanding of what your week looks like. We recommend that you allocate time every Friday afternoon to reviewing the week to come and getting things in order. It may seem like a drag doing this on a Friday but discipline sets you free. It's actually cathartic to log off on a Friday knowing what's in store for the following week. So what does getting your diary in order look like?

Prioritise, prioritise, prioritise

It's easy to find yourself overwhelmed by the number of tasks you need to work through each day. With so much to do, it may feel like you don't even have time to figure out where to start. It may feel like no matter how much you do, you can never get it all done, and this can create a vicious cycle: you get more anxious, more stressed, and this affects your sleep so you have less energy to do all the things you need to do. Don't compare yourself to Elon Musk and assume because he can work maniacal hours and run several global businesses concurrently, you can too. He admits himself that he doesn't recommend working like he does. Our advice is simple. Get out of this busy hustle. The best way to do this is to slow down and prioritise your workload. Write down your tasks for the week ahead, create three categories — *must do, might do, won't do* — and consider the amount of time you'll need to allocate for each task. We recommend writing each task on a Post-it note so it's easy to move them around. Also, if you have a wall/whiteboard you can leave the Post-its up and experience the joy of scrunching them up once each is completed (Brad always misses the bin but by then he doesn't mind). Your list could look something like table 3.1.

If you're doing this right, you shouldn't have more than one or two items in your 'must do' list, three to four in your 'might do' list and lots in your 'won't do' list. Remember, when you prioritise everything, you prioritise nothing. A handy tip here is to allocate 50 per cent more time than you think you'll need to get the job done. If you think something will take you a day, allocate 1.5 days. This way you maximise your chances of completing the task within your working hours, and there's only upside if you get it done quicker. Creating this list also helps you manage expectations with your team and boss. It helps you break free from the busy hustle. Your 'might do's' are exactly that — you might or might not get them done. Your 'won't do' list will be a variety of tasks that can wait until next week or be delegated, or things you've consciously decided not to do.

Table 3.1: task prioritisation

Must do	Time (hrs)	Might do	Time (hrs)	Won't do	Time (hrs)
FY25 business plan	24	Finalise customer loyalty proposal	4	CRM deep dive with IT	2
Sales meeting	2	Review PR and marketing data for business quarter 2	2	People update with HR	2
		Ideation session for new customer product	4	Brown bag session about AI	2
				New business origination ideation call	1
				Review employee onboarding process	2
				Team Xmas party planning	2

Once you have your weekly view, you then need to break the tasks down into chunks of time in your diary. Your 'must do' is your most critical task and once you put this in your diary you should consider it set in stone, locked in. Someone asks to meet at the same time as your 'must do'? 'Sorry, I can't make that time, I'm working on a critical task.' They ask again? The answer is still no. Your 'must do' list ensures that every day you are tackling your most critical task and avoiding being a Busy Idiot or procrastinating. It's easy to procrastinate when you're not invested in what you're doing. Once you've selected your 'must do', if you find yourself picking up your phone and doomscrolling, challenge yourself: 'This is my must do, I've got to get it done.' It reassures you that you're making progress and gives you a sense of accomplishment. But to feel this sense of accomplishment, you've got to make sure you allocate enough time. Thirty minutes isn't enough time to do a critical task; neither is an hour, as it'll take you at least 15 minutes to get into the problem space. Allocate at least 90 minutes to your 'must do'. You might not complete the whole task in that time (depending on what it is), but you'll make a dent and you can return to it the following day.

This is not to say that anything that takes less than 90 minutes is pointless busywork. Customer calls or emails usually take less than 90 minutes and you'll still have plenty of time for all those things. Try to bunch these smaller important tasks together in 90-minute slots, with a five- or 10-minute buffer between them. If you don't add the buffer, what typically happens is that you'll spend the first five minutes of a meeting thinking about the last call and the last five minutes thinking about the next one. That can be pretty stressful, so give yourself time to decompress. Don't spread these tasks across the whole day, though, depleting your headspace to get your 'must do' done. Your 'must do' should give you time to think and do deep work. And don't stress about getting everything done on your to-do list, because that list will never be done. Once you start reflecting on your 'must do' for each day of the week, you'll probably realise that a lot of things on your to-do list really aren't that important. Then you'll feel less busy and less stressed.

Schedule your breaks

A 2022 study compared the productivity of 16 undergraduate students when breaks were not required vs when breaks were taken at regular intervals. Half of the students took five-minute breaks every 20 minutes in the first session, followed by a session with no breaks or a control session where breaks were optional. The other half took breaks in the second session and none in the first. The results were clear: 75 per cent of students were substantially more productive during the sessions with breaks.

This is great news. You can take breaks and be more productive. So schedule them in advance when you're planning your weekly calendar. You've got to eat of course, so make sure you take at least an hour every day for lunch. Working through lunch is not a good idea. You'll likely crash at some point, or be in a foul mood for those late-afternoon meetings. And leave your phone alone during these lunch breaks. Scrolling through your phone won't give your mind the rest it needs. Eating with one hand should only be done if you're eating a delicious Japanese meal with chopsticks.

If you've structured your diary well for the week, you should have clear time allocations for your 'must do' and other key tasks bunched together in 90-minute slots, leaving several spaces in your diary for breaks. When you don't control your diary, break time is normally void. Freeing up some time before your next call or meeting is essential. If you hop from one task to the next without a break, you'll find yourself slowing down and getting increasingly frustrated by your slow pace. When this happens take a break or, if it's near the end of the day, park the task for the following day. It's amazing how something that can feel like an epic struggle at 6 pm becomes a simple task at 9 the next morning. Not all breaks are equal so you need to find what works for you, but it's always good to move, and to move away from your desk. Make time to exercise and get some fresh air, even if it's just a 15-minute walk outside the office.

Finally, just like your computer, you have a finite battery life; sometimes you'll be firing on all cylinders and sometimes everything will feel like a chore. You know if you're a morning person or a night owl. Don't schedule your 'must do' task in the afternoon if that's when you're running slower. Use that time to do something less demanding, like clearing your email or catching up on administrative tasks.

Budget your time

You simply can't control your diary if you don't think carefully about the meetings you organise or accept. Andy Polaine suggests thinking about your calendar as a budget of your time. Let's assume you want eight hours for sleep and eight hours for time with your family and friends. This leaves eight hours for work, and that's plenty if you budget your time well. Just like any budget, the first thing you should do is review your spending. Here hindsight beats foresight. You'll rationalise that all your coming meetings are important, so conduct an audit of your calendar over the previous month. Use a pen and paper, a dummy calendar, an Excel sheet — whatever works — to list all the meetings you attended over the past month, and tally up the totals. If you're in a managerial position, it might look something like table 3.2.

In this mock diary, the manager is losing 5.5 days (more than a week) every month on meetings. Note that with the possible exception of the project review, none of these meetings relate to customer tasks. This is a conservative view; we know of senior managers and leaders who cram their schedules with recurring 1v1 meetings every day. Be very careful of committing to recurring meetings, and reserve them for your closest collaborators who provide you with most value. When meeting with direct reports on a recurring basis, think about the right frequency. Is weekly truly necessary? Recurring meetings usually carve out a huge amount of time with no clear view of how the time will be spent. When you are asked, 'Shall we just put a placeholder in to catch up at this time every week?', your best response is an honest one: 'Sorry, I get asked a lot for regular catch-ups so I just have to decline or I'd do nothing else! But when you have a specific problem or opportunity you want to discuss, just give me a call.' By auditing your diary like this you can reflect on how you're spending your time and whether these meetings are really necessary. If you're not sure, cancel first and reinstate later if you discover that the meeting was needed (this rarely happens). If you are obliged to keep some meetings, such as check-ins with your boss, change the frequency. You'll probably find you have more meaningful conversations when you catch up less frequently.

Table 3.2: a time budget

Meeting name	Purpose	Frequency	Total monthly time (hrs)
Team 1v1s	Informal check in to see how each team member is going	Weekly	16
Weekly team catch-up	Informal check in with the team	Twice weekly	8
Business performance check-ins	Review of business performance	Weekly	4
Project X review	Review of status of Project X	Twice weekly	8
1v1 with Manager	Informal check-in with boss	Weekly	4
1v1 with Finance Manager	Catch-up with finance to review business performance	Fortnightly	2
1v1 catch-up with HR	Informal catch-up to discuss people-related issues	Fortnightly	2
		Total:	**44 hours**

By streamlining your diary, you start to build an accurate picture of how much time you really have for meaningful work. Imagine a scenario where you are asked to work on a project that your manager estimates will take four working weeks. The deadline is set, but you really only have three working weeks, as a week is lost in meetings. What can happen in these situations is that the real work gets pushed to the evenings and weekends, and you feel burnt out, stressed and frustrated. In this scenario, it's not really your boss's fault for setting the deadline in four weeks. It's your fault for not having a clear picture of how much available time you can dedicate to the project. By auditing your diary, you can manage expectations better; in this scenario you could have told your boss, 'I agree this should only take four weeks but unfortunately I have commitments that will take up some of my time, so can we make the deadline five weeks from now?' Meeting overload is the number one symptom of busy idiocy. Audit your calendar, delete meetings and reclaim time. If you're a manager, or the scheduler of a meeting, you're reclaiming time not only for yourself but for your wider team too. It's a virtuous cycle of productivity gains.

Handle conflict with grace

To bring this tip to life, let's check back in with Natalie. After leaving her consulting role, Natalie worked as a Brand Manager for a large beverage company (let's call them BevCo). Natalie worked in BevCo's alco-beverage division, looking after one of BevCo's flagship brands, an easy drinking lager called BevCo Dry. It was Natalie's job to improve BevCo Dry's market share, drive sales and improve brand awareness. Natalie has been with BevCo for five years and over the past two consecutive years narrowly missed out on promotion to Head of Marketing. She was told this year would be her year, if she could grow BevCo

Dry's market share by 0.5 per cent, which she'd done successfully for the previous two years. Natalie felt confident. At the start of the new financial year, however, her boss and champion moved laterally in the firm and a new Chief Marketing Officer (CMO) was appointed. Natalie felt anxious that her promise of promotion might not now be honoured. After speaking with her new boss, though, she was assured she was on the right track, if she just kept doing what she was doing for another 12 months.

Her new boss, Sandra, was keen to make an impact as the new CMO of BevCo's alco-beverage division; it was no secret that the current CEO was nearing retirement and Sandra was in the running as a successor. But she didn't want to just play it safe and hit her numbers. She wanted to invest in different, game-changing projects to put her name in lights. Sandra felt there was a gap in the market for an adult non-alcoholic drink. One that would have other 'functional ingredients' that would make you feel relaxed and jolly, minus the risk of a hangover. Sandra called the project 'Buzz' and set up a think tank to conduct market research to understand the potential size of the prize. Natalie was drafted into this group and told to work with them as a 'plus-one' activity. If you are not familiar with this expression, it's business-speak for 'do it in addition to your day job', which in real terms normally means 'do it in your evenings'.

Natalie was frustrated by this distraction. She felt the non-alco space was already saturated and it conflicted with her interest in improving market share of BevCo Dry lager. Natalie's key performance indicators (KPIs) were all tied to sales of BevCo Dry, and she couldn't see how this project would help her land her overdue promotion. Natalie begrudgingly took part in the working sessions each evening. The team of three conducted some quick customer research, reviewed the competitive landscape and put together a draft business case. In the meantime, sales of BevCo Dry flattened as their direct competitor rolled out a nationwide campaign directed at pubs on the east coast to stock their beer exclusively with special discounts.

Natalie began to resent the working group. Each week they provided a status update to Sandra, who bubbled with energy and enthusiasm for Project Buzz. In week 5, Sandra added some new names to the weekly catch-up, including the CMO of BevCo's soft drink division. On the call, Sandra explained that Project Buzz was incredibly exciting but technically fell under the remit of Julio's soft drink division. Sandra suggested that everyone could work as one joint team to get the product launched, but all revenue would hit Julio's P&L. Natalie was quietly seething. To make matters worse, with everyone on the call, Sandra delegated ownership of Project Buzz to Natalie.

A regrettable exchange

Sandra: 'Natalie, please could you give an update to Julio's team on Project Buzz, and then it would be great if you could continue to run the project and keep both Julio and me updated.'

Natalie: 'Why would I run this project? Someone from Julio's team should, given they'll get all the credit if this is a success. The revenue will hit the soft drinks P&L.'

Natalie's choice of words was boorish. Sandra, with one eye on running the whole company in the near future, took the opportunity to grandstand...

Sandra: 'Natalie, this is exactly the sort of attitude I will never tolerate. We are one company and everyone at BevCo should be working together to make this company the best *it could possibly be regardless of what division you're in. A rising tide lifts all boats!'*

Natalie knew that any success from Project Buzz would be recognised on Julio's P&L and any promotions or pay rises would be distributed among his team. She felt she'd been dealt a sucker punch. She thought back to her disagreement with Gary and the impact that had on her career at the time. She apologised and promised to head the working group and provide regular updates.

A sliding doors moment

Natalie had reason to feel aggrieved for being asked to work on a project that she stood little to gain from. Any intangible goodwill from Sandra would have been offset by the extra workload and her failure to meet the KPIs that her promotion depended on. Her frustration was exacerbated by her feeling that she should have been promoted already. Working the extra hours, she'd become increasingly irritable. All of these factors conspired against Natalie's desire to take part in the project, maintain her new boss's goodwill and get to work on meeting her KPIs to secure promotion. Natalie went into the meeting riled up, and hearing that Julio's team would inherit her work and (in her mind) get all the credit was the final straw. She blew up, and blew her chances of navigating her way off the project. Had Natalie been thinking straight (more on this later), the exchange could have played out completely differently.

Sandra: 'Natalie, please could you give an update to Julio's team on Project Buzz, and then it would be great if you could continue to run the project and keep Julio and me updated.'

Natalie: 'Sure, happy to give an update and it's great that Julio and team are joining the team. However, could I make a suggestion that someone from Julio's team picks up the baton from here? The truth is that they have more experience than I do in the non-alco sector and would be best placed to make this project successful. I also don't want to take my eye off the revenue growth of BevCo Dry, which is a key priority for the company. Does that make sense?'

Sandra: 'Hmm, that does make sense, but I do think of this as an adult beverage, so we need some involvement.'

Natalie: 'Sure. I'll do a thorough handover and Julio's team can call me whenever they need my help.'

Sandra: 'Okay, sounds like a plan. Julio, who do you want to assign to take ownership of the program?'

By keeping her cool, Natalie is now free to concentrate on her day job and path to promotion. Sure, Julio's team might call her now and again, but she'll be able to manage requests in line with her other priorities now she's not ultimately accountable.

Take a breath (or several)

In two decades of working, we can't recall a single confrontation that we're proud of, even in discussions where we've made the stronger argument and gained the upper hand. There's nothing to gain from belittling a colleague, manager or client. And every dispute, which felt significant at the time, seems entirely unimportant in hindsight. We are all responsible for our own emotional responses, no matter how frustrating the circumstance might be. Responses like Natalie's happen every day and cause untold unnecessary stress. Even with the extra workload, Natalie should have controlled her diary and allowed herself time to think and to compose herself. Instead of allowing her emotions to escalate, she could have reflected on why she's annoyed and then taken steps to remedy the situation. With careful thought and a considered approach to her boss, she might have been excused from the distracting working group before the fateful exchange.

You know inherently when you're entering a stressful situation, a meeting you don't want to join. Your heart rate increases, you feel a little hot; if it's a really stressful situation, you may even feel sick. If you enter a meeting stressed, you're unlikely to get the outcome you want. So take a deep breath, or several. Remind yourself that this is not as important as you think it is.

'Fives' is a good way to quickly recalibrate and bring yourself back into a calm state. Look around the room you're in and count five colours silently to yourself. Alternatively, scan the room and count five shapes. When you're in the heat of the moment and you feel your blood boiling, take heed of Dale Carnegie's timeless advice: *control the space between the stimulus and your action*. If you can't collect your thoughts, hold your tongue and ask if you can think about the request and come back to the group. Write down this old adage and stick it on a Post-it note on your desk: *Act in haste, repent at leisure*.

Be careful with 'yes'

With those words still echoing in your head, be careful saying yes too often. It's so easy to say yes. No is loaded with potential conflict. We sympathise. Part of being human is we crave social acceptance: we like to be liked; we need to be needed. In chapter 4, we discuss oxytocin and the need for social connection. 'Yes' is inextricably linked with that. We don't want to offend our social connections with no. However, you must get comfortable with saying no. We've heard some pretty shoddy advice over the years. Joff recalls one Senior Manager at a large consulting firm telling a junior analyst, 'Just say yes to everything — it's the best way to build a great reputation.' We've learned that those people who say yes to everything early on never learn the knack of saying no. We've seen these people move through the ranks by being hard workers with good attitudes, only to hit a ceiling when they try to move into leadership positions: 'He's more of an order taker than a leader', 'He's a good doer but he's not very strategic'. It's true you may have to say yes more often when you're starting out (to gain experience on what you should be saying no to), but you need to develop the critical skill of saying no from the start.

Developing the ability to handle conflict with grace will help you get to a place where you can say no and your counterpart will understand why and accept it. Most important, don't say yes if it feels wrong in your gut, even if you're being pressured. Perhaps you don't have the right skill set, or you know you won't be able to afford sufficient time to complete the task. These are legitimate reasons, so don't blurt out a reluctant yes. The worst thing you can do is say yes (knowing you should have said no) then have to backtrack later. You may have been cornered by an aggressive manager, but hold your ground. They'll use it against you later: 'Hold on, you said you could help and now you're saying no? I can't find someone else now, the project is in flight.' You're trapped. They may have forced you to say yes, but ultimately you still said it. If you encounter a pushy manager who apparently won't take no for an answer, defer commitment. Tell them you can't make a decision right now and you'll get back to them. By doing this you've paved the way to a no later.

Start with the heart

We're not advocating that you approach all work with scepticism and be seen as uncooperative and negative. That's not going to help your career or happiness at work. It's good to treat all initial requests for help positively. Tell yourself, *Wow, it's great that they want my help*. Conversely, perhaps no-one wants your help. This is isolating and normally means you're in the wrong job. So treat all requests for help with curiosity and warmth. Even if you suss out from the meeting invite that it's likely something you'll need to say no to, don't act like a jerk, for example by just hitting 'Decline' without a cover note. Being a jerk doesn't get you to a no quicker; in fact, it often leads to unnecessary escalations that take up more time. If you recognise straight away that the meeting isn't relevant for you, decline with a kind but firm note: 'Thanks for thinking of me but sadly I don't think I can help with this, I specialise in *xxx*. David's team works in this space — I can intro you if that's helpful?'

When you're in a meeting and someone asks for your help, put yourself in their shoes. They've got a task they need help with and they're anxious to get it going. Even if you're dealing with someone who is aggressive, don't reply in kind. Be kind and firm. If they're super pushy, try to marry a can't with a can. If you find yourself just saying no, no, no, you're likely going to find yourself in a hostile exchange. In her imagined positive exchange, Natalie explained she couldn't lead the project but she could be on the end of the phone to help. The key is to make sure you're committing to something you genuinely can help with. If you can't see a way you can add value, be kind and firm: 'I don't see how I can help, but if the project scope changes please do let me know.' They might not like this answer, but in hindsight even a superior will recognise that you showed maturity and held your own.

If 'marrying a can't with a can' doesn't work, tie your no to their objectives. If you embrace the request to help with kindness and curiosity, you'll have a good understanding of what the project is and why you can or can't help. If you feel like you're not suited (even if they think you are), it's hard to defend against a no when you position it against their objectives: 'Thanks for sharing the project background. It's super interesting and I completely understand we have to get this right. Sadly, I don't have the skills in *xxx*, which are absolutely critical. I could do *xxx*, but this isn't relevant for this project and would distract from your target objectives.'

Starting with the heart is a great default mindset; however, as the old saying goes, fool me once, shame on you; fool me twice, shame on me. In the same way you might not keep meeting up with a friend who was rude to you, treat your colleagues the same. Keep a busy idiot list in your head and be on guard when they come knocking. You can try to ignore these requests, but if they are persistent, often asking some simple qualification questions will help. Before jumping into a meeting, send a message: 'Sorry, I'm time-poor right now. Can you send me a short brief on what help you need?' Often a busy idiot won't have thought deeply about the task and this simple request will derail them.

If a meeting invite comes through with no agenda, defer acceptance or decline by default. With no agenda, you have no idea what you're signing up for and you shouldn't have to lose 30 or 60 minutes of your time to find out. Further, it's almost always true, when a meeting comes through without an agenda, that the person setting up the meeting hasn't thought deeply about its purpose. Such a meeting is likely to be unstructured and unproductive and result in a follow-up meeting.

When you say yes you're committing your most valuable resource — your time. When you say yes to everything, you're still saying no to several things. You can't do everything and by trying to you'll end up eroding trust and being labelled unreliable. The trick, therefore, is to be super protective of your most valuable resource without becoming unapproachable, unhelpful or unlikable. Say no with warmth and clear reasons, and don't burn bridges.

Build your circle of influence

At the start of this chapter, Natalie found herself suckered into a meaningless project by her superior, Gary. He wasn't concerned about the low chances of winning the work, he wasn't worried that Natalie didn't have adequate support, and he certainly wasn't going to roll up his sleeves to help. Natalie might have thought it was just bad luck that she got collared. Yet, if you recall, Jess was also tapped on the shoulder to help but she had an alibi. Jess said she could allocate 50 per cent of her time. What that usually means in reality is, 'I have a more important task that I need to prioritise. I'll jump in to help when I can'. While Natalie's frustration grew as she worked long hours on an unprofitable task, Jess felt much calmer with the freedom to jump in and out to focus on her more important work.

Jess's advantage was that she had been with the company for four years and in that time had built a reputation and a network. Whereas Natalie hit the bench, waiting to be told what to do, Jess proactively contacted a Partner she'd previously enjoyed working with to see if she could help. The universe helps people who help themselves. While it's good to keep a busy idiots list in your head, it's just as important to keep a list of high performers. At school it's not good to hang around with the wrong crowd, and the same is true at work. Avoid leaders you perceive to be busy idiots. Find the leaders you love working with, learn from them and proactively seek opportunities to work with them. Finally, don't get too anxious about ghosting or saying no to a busy idiot while fearing they might seek to tarnish your reputation. Providing you work for a good firm, positive feedback from good leaders will usually drown out any grumblings from a busy idiot boss.

Think straight, talk straight

If you remember only four words from this book, make it these. Get clarity of your thoughts and communicate them simply. This will save you more time in your professional career than anything else. This is a rare skill that we think is becoming rarer as we minimise our F2F social interactions (as we outlined in chapter 2). We're so busy we don't take the time to think before we speak, which can cause confusion, anger, frustration and other negative emotions that are not conducive to making progress.

You may think that you don't need to plan for meetings, that you can just wing it. Maybe you believe you can rely on your 'gift of the gab'. We've been in too many meetings to mention listening to people who love the sound of their own voice, imagining they're oozing charisma, when they're actually losing their audience and their influence. Fewer words are always more powerful than more words, but it takes time and preparation to communicate succinctly. This time is important and needs to be invested. If you don't, chances are you'll find yourself in a follow-up meeting or, worse, regular catch-ups as you try to undo the miscommunication resulting from the first meeting.

Figure 3.1 shows a simple meeting planning template to help you think straight and talk straight. It can be completed by you regardless of whether you are chairing the meeting.

Desired outcome

Why is this a problem today?	What are the benefits for the business?

Supporting data

What not to say

Key points

Figure 3.1: TSTS meeting plan template

It's designed for your reference, not necessarily to be shared with all attendees.

Let's explore a mock scenario. A Head of Marketing at a small accounting software business has set up a meeting with his boss, the CEO, to get preapproval for a marketing budget for the next 12 months. Currently the Head of Marketing has to make a business case for each individual spend, set up a meeting to explain the rationale and await a decision, which often entails a follow-up meeting. He's frustrated that he can't get on and do his job. His CEO is a busy woman who doesn't have a marketing background. She rarely says no to requests and just holds things up unnecessarily. He's frustrated by being micromanaged and thinks the process is dumb. However, he's unlikely to achieve his objectives if he conveys that message. Figure 3.2 illustrates how the TSTS template could be utilised.

If you follow the meeting template, you can probably sense the Head of Marketing's frustration. *What it's about is never really what it's about.* The Head of Marketing is not too concerned about the extra spend and ROI.

Without taking the time to think straight and talk straight, the Head of Marketing could easily find himself in an emotional exchange about his frustrations. Worse still, his frustration could spill over and he could make it personal. He could tell his boss, 'You're never available.' The old cliché 'it's not personal, it's just business' is recited when someone gets the upper hand on a business deal. Remember those words when you're trying to think straight and talk straight. Don't make business issues about individuals or personalities; always ladder up to actual business problems or opportunities. Taking the time to think through what you must *not* say is important, as things can slip out when you're under pressure, in the heat of the moment.

Desired outcome

Get approval from my boss for a 12-month marketing budget of $500k

Why is this a problem today?

- Lots of wasted time spent on approval meetings
- Missed opportunities for events and campaigns due to speed of approvals
- Losing out on early bird or last-minute event discounts due to speed of approvals
- Hard to get into a regular cadence of marketing activities due to inconsistent approval durations

What are the benefits for the business?

- Net $ saving on marketing activities
- Better ROI on marketing activities
- Time saved for team and boss to focus on more critical tasks

Supporting data

- Spent an extra $15 000 on events over the year by missing out on discount deals or early-bird specials
- ROI on marketing activity 30 per cent higher in Q1 ($250k) when we got quick approval for all activities vs Q2 when we had to wait for approval and bunch activities into the back end of the quarter

What not to say

- You are never available and you often bump my meetings
- I'm better qualified to make these decisions myself; I don't get any new ideas from the approval meetings
- I should be allowed my own budget, it's ridiculous that I don't at my level

Key points

- I think there's an opportunity to review the way we currently draw down on our marketing budget.
- I would like to suggest that you approve a 12-month spend.
- Doing this will save money as we'll be able to take advantage of early-bird or last-minute deals.
- We'll also be able to set up a cadence of marketing activities, which we've seen results in a better ROI of $250k if we compare Q1 vs Q2.
- Any spend outside of the approved marketing budget will still need your approval as per the current process.
- I'd welcome your thoughts.

Figure 3.2: TSTS meeting plan

In this scenario, the Head of Marketing refers to things the CEO will care deeply about — saving money and making more money. Also, she has a control mechanism as there will be no budget overspend without her approval. Only a boss with major trust issues would say no to this request (see page 78: if it is them and not you, hatch an escape plan) and they'll probably appreciate that you've shown initiative and given them some time back in their diary.

Some readers may be thinking at this point, *Great, so these idiots are telling me to waste more time by filling out a TSTS meeting plan.* That may be how it looks on the surface, but consider the time you'll save if your manager does agree with your point, or the time you will lose if you spend a meeting waffling incoherently. You'll probably end up in another meeting trying to make your point again. We think of the TSTS meeting plan as a guide, and once you've used it a few times you'll probably have the skill down without having to pre-plan it in a form. In the world of psychology we often use written forms to help people use templates that will later become more cognitive and automatic in their thinking.

A final tip on how to think straight and talk straight. A meeting plan will go a long way but there will always be curveballs. When you get dealt one of these, the consultant's answer is to say, 'Let me think about that one and get back to you.' It's not a terrible answer, but it's also not a good one. What that really means is, 'I don't know, I need to find out, which means we'll probably need another meeting.' That's not great but it may be your only option if you don't have an answer, and it's way preferable to trying to make something up on the spot, which erodes trust. However, your chances of knowing the answer increase tenfold with experience and knowledge. It takes time of course, but you set the pace for how quickly you obtain knowledge. So read as much as possible (and thank you for reading this book). Reading teaches you to think on your feet and is an investment forward for those tricky questions that may come down the line. It will help you build credibility and trust and might save you from a follow-up meeting (more on the importance of life-long learning in chapter 5).

Choose how you communicate

As we discussed in chapter 2, we now have a proliferation of tools at our disposal and more to come. Historically, innovation always displaces the incumbent technology — the automobile replaced the horse and cart, the mobile phone replaced the landline, Netflix replaced Blockbuster…you get the idea. This does not always apply in the workplace, where we often have a multitude of tools with overlapping capabilities. In our workplaces, just for comms we use at least three different tools. So how do you manage this? They say a poor workman blames his tools, but we've yet to see a plumber do a good job armed only with a hammer. You need to be deliberate in the tools you choose to communicate with. Stripping away brand names, if you work in a corporate environment, you probably have access to the following ways of communicating:

- instant messaging (IM)

- virtual meeting

- email

- text

- phone call

- face to face.

You no doubt have a preferred tool for communication. If you're under 30, it's probably instant messaging (according to Facebook research, 59 per cent of workers prefer IM to email). Wipro's former CEO, Thierry Delaporte, reported that 10 per cent of his 260 000 workforce don't check email even once a month. Yet, email hasn't died yet and still has a role. Likewise, sometimes you still need to pick up the phone, and sometimes a virtual call just won't cut it and you'll need to meet face to face. When deciding which form of communication is best, rules or frameworks aren't particularly helpful, as every workplace culture is different. You can communicate effectively or poorly no matter what tool you use. Let's take email as an example.

Imagine a Program Manager at a digital agency is overseeing the delivery of a new website for a large retail customer (let's call them Retail World). Unfortunately, the project has encountered some difficulties and the client is asking for a financial rebate. The Program Manager sympathises with the client but needs to get internal approval from three different leaders within the business. She intends to discuss the matter over the phone but needs to send an email to provide context.

A bad email from the program manager

Hi xxx, xxx and xxx,

I hope you're all well.

Unfortunately, we need to get on the phone ASAP as Retail World is very angry with our delivery of their new site, and to be honest I don't blame them. Jim and Suresh have been super difficult to work with and we've had multiple complaints all the way through about their unprofessionalism. Have you seen their work? It's not great.

The website should have functionality to let people set up an account, as promised in the statement of work, but that's not been done. There was also supposed to be a virtual assistant, but that doesn't work at all. The client doesn't like the navigation bar either, or the search display function. Also, they haven't followed Retail World's brand guidelines so the look and feel of the site is all wrong.

What sort of rebate do we typically offer clients? I recommend we give 50 per cent at least to maintain the relationship.

Could you all please provide some times to chat ASAP? I need to get back to Retail World this week. Alternatively, just let me know if I can offer 50 per cent so I can try to sort this out.

Thanks,

xxx
Program Manager

This email is bad on many levels. Firstly, the language is too informal and emotive for this situation. If this were a real scenario, I would assume that the Program Manager sent this in haste after a difficult conversation with the client. Never send an email in haste. Remember: 'Act in haste, repent at your leisure.' If you write an email and you're not sure about sending it, don't. If an hour has passed and you still want to send it, don't send it. No-one regrets not sending an email. So if in doubt, if your gut is twisted up, sleep on it and forget it. If someone is demanding a response, pick up the phone. I'm surprised smartphones are still called phones, as for many people that's no longer the primary purpose of the device. Using the phone is in danger of becoming a forgotten art as we snap and swipe instead of chit and chat. This is a problem. Email and instant messaging might promise to save you time but written words can be interpreted in multiple ways and sometimes you need to get on the phone to avoid a busy back and forth.

But we digress. The second issue with this email is that there's a number of questions but the Program Manager doesn't specify who they are addressed to. It's likely here that no-one will answer these questions, or that a busy email chain kickstarts and everyone will. The Program Manager starts the email by saying they need to meet to discuss the matter but then proceeds to tell her superiors what they should do (offer a rebate). The Program Manager reinforces that she doesn't really value their input by suggesting at the end that they just give her approval to offer the rebate. Finally, remember *it's not personal, it's just business.* The Program Manager makes it personal by robustly sharing her opinion on the quality of her colleagues' work. A good tip here when writing an email is to imagine that it's inadvertently sent to everyone in the company. If that mistake happened, would you still be okay with it? If not, don't put your comments down in writing. Address any sensitive matters on a call or face to face. In this scenario, there's a chance that the email is forwarded to the colleagues she's criticising. This could easily start a game of he said/she said and make it difficult to reach a good outcome for the client quickly. Finally, the email is just too long and unstructured. A busy executive might glaze over an email like this, and the Program Manager won't get the help she needs.

A good email from the Program Manager

Hi xxx, xxx and xxx,

I hope you're all well.

Unfortunately, I've just received a call from Retail World and they're unhappy with our performance on the project. In summary,

- *the client has raised complaints on three separate occasions about poor communication and team members being late for important review meetings*

- *we have failed to deliver key scope items (e.g. the virtual assistant) within the time frame*

- *they are refusing to sign off elements we have delivered such as the homepage navigation*

- *they have lost faith in our ability to deliver this project in full and are requesting a financial rebate.*

I will find time in your diaries for us to discuss this in more detail and explore options on how we can get the project and relationship back on track.

Thanks,

xxx
Program Manager

In this second email, the Program Manager uses half the number of words to explain the situation. Bullet points are great as they allow you to highlight key points in a list; use them in email comms as much as possible. They stop you from writing a letter, which should be reserved for bills and romance. In this email, the Program Manager also doesn't make it personal by naming and blaming individuals, or sharing her opinion over email. There's also no need to ask questions. Everything will be discussed on the call. Finally, she shows initiative and takes the burden away from her superiors by offering to find a time that works to meet. By sending this email rather than the former, the Program Manager is already on her way to getting the advocacy she needs to bring the client back on side.

Be polite when using weapons of mass distraction

Imagine you're working in the office and you can't find a document. You think your colleague will know where it is but he's in a meeting. Nevertheless, you barge into the meeting unannounced and shout, 'Hey David!' You stand there awkwardly for five minutes but there's no response. (David's in a meeting, after all.) So you raise your voice again: 'David, can you share our sustainability report?' David ignores you again so you leave the meeting room. Five minutes later you barge back in and shout, 'David, please. I need this in the next 10!' Exasperated, David leaves the meeting and shows you where to find the document — in the folder clearly marked 'Sustainability report'.

This may seem like a silly example — you'd never interrupt your colleagues so rudely. Yet, this is exactly how many of us use the instant messaging platforms that have infiltrated every workplace. They have become weapons of mass distraction. It's okay to ask for help. You should never feel like you have to solve problems alone, but this doesn't mean you need to bother your colleagues with every trivial problem. Take a moment to think before you interrupt someone. Do I really need this person's help? Then ask, do I really need this person's help *right now*? Few matters are really urgent enough to require an instant message. You may think you aren't doing anything wrong by using instant messaging as your default channel. Your colleague can still choose to respond or not in their own time. While this is true, instant messaging platforms come with a loaded expectation. The clue is in the name, *instant* messaging, and the loaded expectation that the receiver will reply immediately. When you say, 'Hi David', you're really saying please answer me *now* so I can get your help with something *now*. It's the same when you send a text. One could infer that your intent is to get around your colleague's email inbox and raise your request to the top of their list. That could be conceived as a pretty rude way to behave!

If you truly need help, be polite if you're using instant messaging in the same way you would when approaching someone in person. For example, don't lead with, 'Hi David', which is riddled with endless possibilities about what you want and how much of your colleague's time you might need. Instead, opt for, 'Hey David, it's not urgent but when you get a sec, pls can you send me that sustainability report. Sorry, I just can't find it!'

Take the time to learn people's communication preferences too. If email is their preferred method of communication, respect that and send an email instead of an instant message.

Stay in holiday mode and do nothing

The fourth law in Deepak Chopra's 'seven spiritual laws of success' tells us that we can do nothing and accomplish everything. This might sound ludicrous if you're caught in a busy trap — you're working every hour and getting nowhere and somehow doing nothing is going to help? Well, we'd argue that yes it will. Sometimes the less you do, the more you'll achieve. Doing fewer things but with intention is far better and more productive than doing a lot of things mindlessly. If you're doing lots of things mindlessly, you're likely only achieving burnout and stress. You'd be better off doing nothing.

Think about the last time you went on holiday for more than a week. Often for the first few days you're still in busy mode and continue to check and respond to emails, maybe even foolishly make the odd call. By the second week of the holiday you've finally started to unwind and stop obsessing about work. When you get back to the office you feel relaxed, calm and less emotionally invested in your day job. You also have 100+ unread emails. What do you do? Option one is you start at the bottom of your inbox and respond to every unread email. As you work your way up, you realise that some of the issues have been resolved and you have to send more emails to the tune of 'Sorry, pls disregard'. Congrats, you're back to being a busy idiot. If you resist the urge to respond right away, you'll find that 80 per cent of the issues are resolved without your input, leaving you with only a couple of critical matters requiring your attention. Imagine if work was always like this, if you could successfully avoid the noise and just focus on the 20 per cent that requires your focus.

So how do you stay in holiday mode and do nothing without being seen to be unresponsive or idle? First, slow down. You've got your calendar for the week sorted, and you know what your 'must do' tasks are, so everything else can wait. No-one dies if you don't respond to an email immediately. So wait. You'll be surprised how many problems are resolved or disappear without the need to stress, fret and dive straight into fire-fighting mode. Second, if you're cc'd don't respond. The email isn't directed at you. You might think you can wade in and save the day, but you have other critical things you've committed time to.

If you're a super responsive person (a polite way of saying you're probably a busy idiot), you might be anxious about the thought of changing your working style. You might even get FOMO from suddenly being left out of conversations as work tasks move on (which is not all your fault — see chapter 4). Quite simply, there's no need to be anxious. Any task that is truly important will be followed up with an email or call. You'll be amazed how much time you'll save waiting for these follow-ups; most tasks aren't critical and resolve themselves. However, you might feel guilty that you're not firing on all cylinders. We would recommend you go cold turkey to circuit break your busyness traits. Block out an hour a week in your diary to do nothing. Literally nothing. Don't use the time to read, to catch up on admin or to get ahead on your Christmas shopping. Do nothing. If you're familiar with meditation, try sitting with your eyes closed; try not to think, just observe your breathing and listen to the sounds around you. If you do this regularly, you'll realise two things. First, nothing of note happened in the hour you were absent; in fact, you'll probably find that some supposedly urgent tasks resolved themselves. Second, you'll have a clearer mind, a mind that is starting to break out of its responsive, unproductive busy addictive traits.

As you now operate in holiday mode, the last thing you want to do is spend time with colleagues who annoy you. This may be your boss or a peer who's always asking you to do things urgently. I don't recommend you say this to them directly (though you could if feeling particularly bold), but tell yourself this when these requests happen: *Your lack of planning is not my emergency!* Don't take part in their busy games. Truly important tasks rarely come out of nowhere but require thought, work and planning. Over two decades we've developed a strong busy idiot radar. These people who fly by the seat of their pants, soak up your time and rarely get results. In our first interaction with a colleague, we judge them not on their credentials but on how they present information and how deliberative they are. Is this person going to do what they say? Are they going to add value? Sometimes it can be hard to tell from an initial meet and greet, but once we're burned we move the person to our busy idiots list and treat all future requests for help with suspicion. This may seem harsh or unkind, but remember that your time is your most important resource. Always handle these conflicts with grace, but keep a sharp eye on these people and when their next request comes, back away, wait it out and don't play their busy games. Stay in holiday mode and do nothing.

If it's them and not you, hatch an escape plan

The moments that stand out for Joff over his corporate career are not times when he's won a big client contract or delivered a great project. It's not winning awards and getting promotions. The moments that remain vivid in his memory are when he's had to console colleagues in distress. They may be in tears, shaking, completely burned out by the work they've found themselves slaving over day after day, month after month. Joff's reaction is always the same: Can he help them get onto a different project, or into a different area of the business? If not, can he help them find a new job? It may seem unprofessional to actively help someone leave the business you're supposed to be representing, but don't be a professional employee at the expense of being an amateur human being. Also, large corporations often have cultures within cultures. One part of a business might have a great leader and culture, and another not so much. Remember, more often than not you leave your manager, not the company.

By definition, your biggest problem is the one you think about the most. Often when colleagues are in distress, they are facing some sort of emotional crisis. They think they're not good enough; they feel trapped and miserable. We try to remind them that it's just a job. If you have ever moved from one job to another, you'll know how easy it is to forget about the job as soon as you hand in your pass. What seemed so important now seems irrelevant, and that boss that drove you mad day in, day out is relegated to a mere cutout figure. If these tips don't help you get control of your life and provide a barrier from busywork, we recommend you schedule a meeting with your boss and use the Think Straight, Talk Straight framework. If your boss dismisses this, you could go to your boss's boss — what have you got to lose?

If none of these approaches work, perhaps you're working in an organisation with a culture that doesn't value you, so it may be time to leave. We recommend you start looking for another job before giving notice. Mentally quitting your stressful job and starting to focus on a role that offers a more promising work–life balance can be cathartic in itself. But always leave with grace and don't get into a war of words with your boss, as much as you might feel tempted. It's not the movies, and you'll regret a heated exchange on leaving. Ask for advice from people in your network and you'll be surprised how many people will be willing to help you find your next role. However, there's no shame in pulling the pin if you just need to get out and you've got the financial security to do so. Your time is your most valuable asset and you'll never know when your time's up, so don't waste your life being miserable in a job you hate.

How to manage your busy boss

1. Control your calendar

- Plan your calendar at least a week in advance.

- Identify and prioritise your 'must do' tasks.

- Schedule your breaks.

- Budget your time.

 Top tip: Remember, your calendar is the greatest defender of your time.

2. Handle conflict with grace

- Take a breath, or several!

- Reflect on the conflict and identify steps to mediation.

- Quickly quieten your mind by using the 'fives' technique.

 Top tip: Display this piece of wisdom on your desk: Act in haste, repent at leisure.

3. Be careful with 'yes'

- Start with the heart, and treat requests for help with curiosity and warmth.

- Marry a can with a can't.

- Tie your no to their objectives.

- Keep a mental busy idiots list.

- Decline to attend a meeting with no agenda.

- Build your circle of influence.

 Top tip: Say no with warmth and logic, and don't burn your bridges.

4. Think straight, talk straight

- Fewer words are more powerful than many words, but it takes time and preparation to be succinct.

- Use the TSTS meeting plan to ensure a desired outcome from meetings.

- Read widely—it teaches you to think on your feet!

 Top tip: Always ladder up to business problems.

5. Choose how you communicate

- Be deliberate with the tools you choose and how you communicate.

- Remember, no-one regrets not sending an email.

- Use bullet points in emails to be succinct.

- Be courteous and respect your colleagues' communication preferences.

 Top tip: Whichever channel you use, keep your work communications clear, to the point, succinct and respectful.

6. Stay in holiday mode and do nothing

- Slow down; you'll be surprised how many issues resolve themselves.

- Block out an hour a week in which to do nothing.

- Don't take part in busy games. Remember, 'Your lack of planning is not my emergency.'

 Top tip: Aim to do a few things with intention rather than a lot of things mindlessly.

7. If it's them and not you, hatch an escape plan

- The biggest problem is the one you think about the most.

- Ask for help from your network.

- Always leave with grace.

 Top tip: Don't waste time, your most valuable asset, working unhappily for a busy boss!

CHAPTER 4

The challenges of loneliness and disconnection

We have delved into the dark arts of persuasive design and how they keep us distracted through the various apps, games and messenger platforms on the screens that surround us. We've considered how to audit and harvest tech in a healthy and sustainable way, and the steps you can take to manage your busy boss, calendar and the chaos of your workplace. We haven't yet explored the nitty-gritty neuroscience behind busyness in the modern workplace. This chapter will help you understand how to manage tech in the workplace and within your teams.

Here are two claims we hear a lot:

'I only do meetings online and haven't seen my work colleagues face to face for months.'

(Who cares?)

'I work with multiple devices that are constantly pinging me because I'm a master of multitasking!'

(Uhh... maybe, but unlikely.)

Neural pathways: use 'em or lose 'em

The impact of screens on our neural pathways is complex. Brad sat down with his research lab partner Professor Wayne Warburton (Macquarie University, Australia) to see if he could explain it in layperson terms. Having been a plumber in a former life before deciding he might just go out and try this academic thing, he is pretty gifted at putting the complex into everyday language.

Wayne explains that neural development in a baby is 'busy'. Infant brains wire up in response to everything they experience and rapidly build connections. At age three a child has two to three times as many neural connections as an adult, and their brain uses twice as much fuel. By this age many brain structures are nearly complete — in particular those that handle automatic processes like breathing and heartbeat, feeling emotions and laying things down in memory. The cortex, however, where our higher functions such as thinking, focusing, planning, managing our feelings, movement and much more take place, won't be fully functioning until our mid to late twenties or later.

In the tween years (from around age 10 to 12) we move into a consolidation or neural pruning phase during which we start to rid our brain of anything we don't use, while the things we do use stay wired in. Think of it as the ultimate clean-out of your email inbox or desktop.

Over our lives our brains are fairly plastic and changeable, even if less amenable to change in the adult years. In our adult years we are more selective about what we commit to memory. We can always rewire existing neural pathways, although it takes serious effort.

Understand the science behind neural pruning

The more time we spend on devices, and chasing our tails in unproductive meetings and disrupted work, the more we are prone to losing our in-real-life (IRL) skills. Consider the core social and communication skills required to participate in an office meeting or a team-building event. They can be broken down into micro skills, including reading facial expressions, body language, social positioning, tone of voice and the list goes on. If we don't practise these skills IRL, we lose both the skill and the neural pathway. This is not an indictment on WFH or hybrid work, but it is a wake-up call of sorts. If an organisation offers that model for its workforce, that's great! There are many advantages. But the question for HR, managers and the CEO is how do we keep our people connected in the real world?

Virtual meetings don't replicate the same neural pathways (the business world calls them 'soft skills'). Does that person have the soft skills for responding to emotional or social situations to lead in their organisation? Does our team have the soft skills to have that hard conversation with their team or manager? Can they respond to having to manage someone's performance or to give a team member emotional support?

Soft skills don't come naturally to everyone, and they are often the hardest to improve. You can't tick it off after a 30-minute online module. But given our neural pruning in this age of technology, we have to ask ourselves if we are headed backwards in exchange for a zero-commute week.

We should note this is not just the domain of the workplace. If screens and technology impact the average person's personal and family time, we have to ask ourselves what neural pathways and soft skills are being pruned in the process?

Compare different workplace models through a neuroscience lens

Neural pathways and pruning are not the only factor when considering the questions, 'Is work from home (WFH) better than hybrid? and 'Is hybrid better than face to face (F2F)? This could be the subject of a stand-alone book! The fact is the rapid change in technology means neuroscience struggles to keep up with the benefits and risks, but we'll touch on a few key areas to consider.

Oxytocin — why your real-world social interactions feel better than online ones

We know, this is the second neurochemical we've introduced, but stay with us — we're not going too deep! For anyone who isn't familiar with it, oxytocin is a chemical that is associated with social connection. It is released in any social interaction, be it online, video, messaging or IRL.

The problem is, a primary driver of oxytocin is physical touch or physical proximity. When we interact with people face to face we get a hit of oxytocin that can't be replicated on a video call or using another messaging tool. In her fantastic book *The Village Effect*, Susan Pinker explains how oxytocin is a primary driver for building trust within teams and groups. It also helps keep us calm when we're stressed. (Is there anything oxytocin can't do!) It doesn't take a neuroscientist to tell you teams and organisations with higher levels of oxytocin are likely to be happier and more productive.

We need to consider our balance between WFH and in-person physical interaction (whether in the office, at lunch with a friend or visiting a client for coffee) and how we plan to maintain our oxytocin levels in the workplace.

Zoom fatigue: how video meetings can impact your productivity

We are not sure how poor old Zoom got lumped with this tag! Maybe it's a sign of its success as the most recognisable video conferencing platform. But we are of course talking about all platforms and methods of video conferencing. For those new to the term, it refers to a feeling of lethargy or listlessness after using video conferencing tools that can be felt directly after the event or even the next day.

Research has found that people new to an organisation suffer most from Zoom fatigue, as their brain works overtime to present the best version of themselves, inhibiting their ability to take in new information. Other studies have indicated that less Zoom fatigue is reported by those who have the camera turned off. Perfect, so you're telling me the answer is simply to turn the camera off? Well, yes and no. It will certainly help with reducing fatigue, but you'll lose all the facial expressions, body language and other social cues we established are needed for our neural pathways to maintain soft skills!

On a genuinely positive note, Bennett (2021) found that those who felt higher levels of group belongingness were somewhat protected from the fatigue effects. Once again, neuroscience is often just common sense, but we need to use big words to make ourselves feel important! Simple translation? The more socially connected you feel to your team, the less worried you are about presenting the perfect you on camera.

Social connection and productivity: why we can't get all our social needs met online

We opened this can of worms so we may as well tackle it. The quality of online relationships can be similar to that we develop F2F, but it takes longer to establish. Humour, sarcasm and body language, for example, are easier to detect in F2F interactions. Once again, the research tells us that the level of 'synchrony' (or harmony) in a group (expressed through non-verbal cues) depends on the quality of the existing relationships in that group. There are positives to online or remote work, two of the key ones being less commuting and the opportunity to assemble an Avengers-like team of experts not bound by geography. However, this is offset by the lack of direct human connection. Gruber (2022) reported that people in workplaces dominated by technology missed F2F interactions and the physical closeness of spontaneous social interactions.

It's difficult to measure productivity levels across competing workplace modes. One measure is Collective Intelligence (CI), which assesses a group's ability to come together and effectively communicate to solve a range of problems or tasks. Kordova and Hirschprung (2023) asked groups of three to seven people to participate in a group project task across four different platforms (F2F meetings, Zoom, WhatsApp and working individually). The groups assigned to F2F meetings performed significantly better on the projects than the other groups.

Productivity is also impacted by interpersonal conflicts within the workplace and teams. Kahlow (2020) found evidence for online teams experiencing more conflict than their F2F counterparts and hypothesised this arose from a lack of cohesion, trust and leadership in establishing group norms.

What's the solution? Theoretically, if you have a team with established social norms and trust, then collaborating online is productive. We share a practical toolkit to help with this in chapter 5.

In 2020, Brad was working in his clinic, which he continues to do for one or two days a week. It helps him stay connected with the real world of modern families. This was when WFH and the pandemic lockdowns were in full swing and we were all forced to work virtually. Except for health professionals like Brad. He opened his office door one day to see a well-meaning father multitasking on his computer, headphones on, with his young daughter next to him watching YouTube on her phone. The man stood up, holding the laptop so it was still in full view, excused himself from the meeting — 'I just need a quick bathroom break, hang on' — before turning off his camera and microphone. He then proceeded to explain to Brad that he also needed to join a work meeting but would just put himself on mute. He explained, 'I just need to stay on the video with one headphone in…' Brad was stunned. He honestly didn't know what to say as the man ushered his daughter into the office and repositioned himself.

Are we seriously doing a session while this guy is technically in a video work meeting? Even more bizarre when you consider that Brad runs a Screens and Gaming Disorder Clinic.

For Brad, that was the day the lines between work and home became inextricably blurred. There have been countless examples since then. But putting that to one side, he couldn't help but ponder the quality of social connection that kind of work provides for us on a human level. The flip side of that emotional equation: loneliness.

Break out of the loneliness loop

In a recent survey of more than 4000 Australian adults, almost one in three Australians (32 per cent) reported feeling lonely. One in three! How is that possible? We are told technology has brought us all together, connected with a warm digital hug! A prominent Facebook slogan, for example, is 'Facebook helps you connect and share with the people in your life'.

The study went on to find that those who reported high levels of loneliness were less productive at work and less physically active; they were also over four times more likely to suffer from depression and twice as likely to have a chronic disease.

The conclusion? Poor-quality social connections do not fulfil our social needs and will not reduce loneliness.

Professor John T. Cacioppo, at the University of Chicago, was arguably the most influential researcher and thought leader in the field of loneliness and social connection. His 2008 book, *Loneliness: Human Nature and the Need for Social Connection*, along with countless peer-reviewed journal publications may be of even greater value to us today than they were at the time of publication. There is some irony in the fact he published that book the year after the iPhone was released. Perhaps he saw the writing on the wall. Cacioppo writes that loneliness is not an objective state of being alone but rather a subjective experience of *feeling* alone. He uses the term 'genetic thermostat' to explain that for some people loneliness kicks in at a lower threshold than for others. Many people with a high genetic thermostat for loneliness would once have been referred to as natural introverts. Earlier in this chapter we discussed how oxytocin is delivered at higher levels when you socialise F2F. It also helps calm us in these social situations, which means we are less likely to withdraw from social events.

The loneliness loop is a vicious cycle (a negative feedback loop) in which the worse (lonelier) we feel the more likely we are to withdraw and avoid social interactions. Many theorise that the antidote to loneliness is connection, and F2F human connection is better than online connection. But what does this mean for the 32 per cent of Australians who feel lonely, who brave the voluntary office day to find the office mostly empty? Their attempt to break out of the loneliness loop came to nought, with no human interaction (and no oxytocin).

This is the challenge of modern workplace design. Organisations need to continue to offer opportunities for human F2F connection and team building.

Is WFH, hybrid or in-the-office best? Get off the fence!

Time for us to stop dancing around the issue and get off the fence on this one. Let's make our stance clear. We have outlined the concerns and risks of WFH and hybrid, but please don't interpret that as indicating we are squarely on 'team get back to the office'. The reality is both of us work remotely for part of the week and around other humans for the other part. Science tells us we need both.

If you are a remote WFH or hybrid organisation, all is not lost! As we have outlined, you can still enjoy all the benefits of this model as long as you work on the protective factors of trust, social cohesion, establishing group norms and leadership. How do you do that? A quick win is with occasional but regular F2F team-building events. Think of it as a reset of all those oxytocin interactions (no, I'm not suggesting you bring in a speaker who facilitates group hugs and forest bathing). When you think about it, though, old-school team building and socialising are a key to happy and productive teams. Who would have thought! Maybe we're not all AI-driven cyborgs just yet...

The challenges of loneliness and disconnection

....

1. Neural pathways: use 'em or lose 'em

- Neural pathways allow your brain to take short cuts for the soft skills you have practised.

- These pathways fully develop by age two or three before going into a 'use it or lose it' function called neural pruning.

- Neural pruning informs our work and life choices every day.

 Top tip: Practise your social and emotional skills, or your neurological ability to use them in future will decline.

2. The modern workplace debate

- Oxytocin is a neurochemical released with social connection. Physical touch and proximity to others is a major driver of oxytocin that can't be replicated at the same levels by current technology communication platforms.

- Zoom fatigue can be combatted with positive social connection and team cohesion.

- Social connection and cohesion depend on the quality of existing group/team relationships.

- Loneliness is on the increase, despite how constantly 'connected' we are. Evidence suggests this is linked to the reduction of F2F interaction and a consequent decrease in oxytocin.

 Top tip: The success of WFH and hybrid relies on key protective factors in any team: trust, social cohesion, group norms and leadership.

CHAPTER 5

You can't go it alone: how to form productive teams

Tennis is a great sport. Each player plays by the same rules on the same court with the same kind of racquet. It's exhilarating, fast paced and with the introduction of Hawk-Eye technology to settle line calls, the best person always wins. Business isn't tennis. Business is complex and uncertain. There are competing strategies, evolving systems and tools, infinite unforeseen variables, and the hopes and fears of disparate personalities. Then add the unexpected into the mix: a global financial crisis or pandemic. To succeed you need to work well with others, to support your colleagues and to rely on them supporting you. It doesn't matter how efficient you are and how well you manage your time (and your boss), if you can't build a productive team you will struggle to avoid busy traps. Whether you work in an inhouse function, or at an agency or consultancy, this chapter will provide a practical toolkit to help you and your team avoid dysfunction. When your team malfunctions you can become a band of frustrated busy idiots.

Mike the top performer vs his project team

Mike's track record for delivering projects was exemplary. For the past three years he'd played numerous roles on large technology implementation projects, from conducting research into user needs, to working as a business analyst to document delivery. His organisation, a large technology consulting firm (we'll call them Consultio), marked him as a rising star. Just three years into his corporate career, he was promoted to a managerial position. Mike didn't feel like the promotion had come too soon; he felt confident he could lead a team successfully. He always delivered. Mike's first task as a manager was to lead the delivery of a new public-facing website for a large insurance company (we'll call them InsureNow). Mike's team consisted of nine people, five based offshore at the firm's delivery centre in Pune, India. Onshore, in London, Mike was supported by a designer, a business analyst and technology architect. As can be common in large organisations, Mike hadn't previously met any of his new team members.

A rough start ...

The kick-off meeting had already been scheduled with the client by the sales rep, so Mike prioritised getting things ready to make a great first impression. He had a 30-minute 1v1 call with the sales rep, who talked him through a high-level plan, the agreed budget and the time frames. Mike had some reservations about the plan and thought some of the activities up front felt rushed. The sales rep told Mike to 'change the plan as you see fit, provided the project is delivered within time and budget'. The rep added that he wouldn't be able to make the kick-off call, so he'd let Mike take it from here. Mike got to work on his kick-off meeting agenda. He sent an invite to the team asking them to 'reach out if they had any questions'.

On the day, Mike met his onshore team, the designer, BA and technology architect, for a coffee in the lobby 30 minutes before the meeting. They had just rolled off other projects and confessed they didn't know much about the project. Mike was unfazed and told them he would lead the meeting and they could jump in where necessary. The rest of the team, comprising a scrum-master and developers, would dial into the meeting. They would be meeting with InsureNow's Head of Technology and Head of Marketing, plus respective members of their teams.

The meeting did not go to plan. First, his colleagues offshore left their cameras off, which didn't build confidence with the client. One of his team members, when asked to introduce himself and his role on the project said he wasn't sure what he would be doing as he was double-booked on another project. He 'could maybe start in a couple of months if that would work?' Mike's confidence was shaken. He deflected and moved on to the project plan. Before he could get into explaining the activities, however, InsureNow's Head of Technology commented that the plan looked markedly different from the one agreed on during the sales process. Mike explained that the plan was now more robust as it allowed more time for upfront design exploration, but he was quickly shot down by InsureNow's Head of Marketing, who explained they had already completed extensive design work internally. They quizzed him on whether he had spoken with the sales rep and understood the key aims of the project.

From this point Mike struggled to regain control. They discussed risks and project governance, but he received little feedback from InsureNow's team on these items. They were concerned about the plan and whether the team were committed to the project. InsureNow's Head of Marketing asked Mike curtly to come back ASAP with a new plan and a date for a rearranged kick-off meeting. Later that day, Mike received an angry call from the sales rep, who reported that the client was thinking about pulling the project but he'd managed to 'smooth things over'. When Mike replied that they'd agreed he could change the project plan, the sales rep hit back, 'I meant you could tweak the project, not change the whole bloomin' plan!'

Like pulling teeth

'It's like pulling teeth,' Mike moaned to his girlfriend that night. He had produced a super-detailed plan, with clear lines of accountability for each activity. He was following agile project principles meticulously. This included a stand-up meeting every afternoon to allow the full team (onshore and offshore) to discuss what each team member was working on and to call out any blockers. Each team member nodded that they knew what they had to do and claimed there were no blockers. Before each sprint Mike agreed on the backlog (the list of items in scope for a two-week period) with the client and the team. Yet, with every sprint they failed to deliver the items in scope. Every week Mike had to send a project status update to the client and flag that the project was running behind schedule. This is not atypical on large delivery programs, but unfortunately for Mike he couldn't explain to the client why the project was running behind schedule. His team said everything was fine but continued to miss deadlines. With no rationale for delays, Mike couldn't charge the client for the overrun on the project. To compound these issues, the client asked for a daily 8.30 am meeting to review progress and flag issues. To prepare for this meeting, Mike had to schedule an additional meeting with the team at 11 pm every night to review work done and understand blockers.

Mike also started to get heat internally. With the project's profit margin dwindling, it was highlighted as a project at risk. This meant Mike now had to attend a weekly review meeting with his superiors to report back on progress, delays and profit projections. This also meant completing another reporting template, in addition to his client status update. Mike worked 14-hour days for four months straight. The project was supposed to be completed within six months but after month four the client decided to complete the project internally and terminated their contract. Mike felt dejected and cursed his luck for getting assigned this as his first project. He blamed the sales rep for not giving a full briefing, the team for being unprofessional and the client for introducing additional meetings that slowed the team down. Internally, Mike's status in the firm was updated, and the 'rising star' now had a black mark against his name.

What went wrong?

You might think Mike got dealt a bad hand. That he should have been supported better by his firm. That he should have got a proper briefing from the sales rep, and that it wasn't his fault his team underperformed. We would argue that this way of thinking is reductive. An old boss of Joff's used to recite, 'Blame is the final refuge of the beaten scoundrel'. When you determine that nothing is your fault and there's nothing you could have done, you accept that you are a passive victim.

If you are a passive victim, you are destined to the fate of a busy idiot. This became Mike's fate. He worked harder and longer hours but couldn't get the project on track. He ended up in more meetings, with mounting administrative and reporting obligations. Mike could have learned from the tips in chapter 3 and respectfully said no to some of these meetings. Ultimately he couldn't find a way to get his team working productively to meet the project expectations. Read on to learn the tips and tools to ensure you don't find yourself sharing Mike's fate when you're leading teams.

Start as you mean to go on

We've mentioned meetings a lot in this book; busy idiots typically love meetings but that's not to say all meetings are bad. The kick-off meeting is the most important of any new project, whether it's an internal project with your key stakeholders or an externally funded client project. A great kick-off meeting will build trust and set you up for success. Strangely, though, kick-off meetings are often relegated to some sort of banal, 'tick-the-box', 45- to 60-minute session. In these kick-off meetings (which are all too typical) the Project Manager produces a slide deck with the following agenda:

1. Introductions — 5 mins

2. Project plan — 20 mins

3. Risk log — 10 mins

4. Governance (meetings and reporting) — 10 mins

5. Dependencies (what we need to get started) — 10 mins

6. Any questions? — 5 mins.

Looks dull, doesn't it? And it is. A project has just been signed off or funded, and everyone is excited to get going — then a dull kick-off. It's the ultimate buzzkill. Typically, there's very little conversation in these meetings. There's hardly any time for introductions or questions, and there's no real time to discuss any of it. It's a kick-off meeting in name only. Yes, it marks the start of a new project, but the project hasn't *really* been kicked off. The team hasn't gelled yet. They might not know each other; that will now have to happen over the early weeks of the project. In chapter 4, we covered social connection and the productivity of teams, and how important it is to establish trust and cohesion, especially if you are going to be working hybrid or WFH. A 60-minute kick-off meeting may seem efficient but you shouldn't confuse speed with progress. A more extended kick-off process paves the way for better project success and productivity. Figure 5.1 shows a better framework for kicking off projects:

Figure 5.1: a better framework for kicking off projects

The basics

The basics are the hygiene factors of a project. They cover the essential elements of the project so everyone understands it and their roles in it. First, you have to get aligned as an internal team, so allocate two or three hours for a *project kick-off discussion*. The agenda may look similar to the banal kick-off meeting previously described, but the intent of a project kick-off discussion is completely different, as you welcome questions and feedback throughout (overleaf):

1. Introductions — 30 mins

   - Each person says hi and introduces their role.

2. Project objectives — 30 mins

   - What are the project goals?

   - How are these goals prioritised?

   - What will success look like? How will we measure it?

3. The project plan — 30 mins

   - Walkthrough + discussion

   - Dependencies + assumptions

   - How we'll work

   Break: 15 mins

4. Risks — 45 mins

   - Each person individually documents risks [10 mins]

   - Share back individually with group [10 mins]

   - Prioritise and rank risks as a group [10 mins]

   - Identify mitigations [15 mins]

5. Next steps — 15 mins

Traditional kick-off meetings are about command and control — 'this is what we're doing'; feedback and contributions are not invited. This can set the tone for the whole project, with team members feeling like they can't or shouldn't contribute. In a project discussion meeting you invite all team members to participate, contribute and gain an understanding of the project.

This structure should be repeated with your client(s) or internal stakeholder(s). It may seem odd spending 30 minutes talking about project objectives, given that these have probably been discussed at length during the sales or project sign-off process. However, projects normally have several objectives and these can often be competing. Returning to Mike's project to create a new public-facing website, the goals of the project could have been:

1. Provide a better customer experience.

2. Reduce cost by reducing calls to the contact centre.

3. Improve employee experience by eliminating mundane tasks for contact centre team.

4. Reduce cost by reducing IT debt.

5. Improve innovation, leveraging new cloud-based platform.

Taking time to discuss project objectives and their priority helps with better and faster decision making during the project. In this example, if the project team agree that reducing costs and calls to the contact centre is the number one priority, this will help stakeholders to agree, or at least disagree but commit, on a decision and path forward. Slow decision making kills projects and blows out project time frames and costs.

Similarly, it may feel uncomfortable to discuss risks and potential issues with your client or stakeholder in the very first meeting. However, as in everything in life, it's better to deal with problems (or potential ones) early. Making risk management a co-creation activity invites shared responsibility and awareness around the risks. Plus, risk logs are boring and disengaging. Running a co-creation activity around risk makes it a generative, creative exercise. It means that when issues arise, there's a better shared understanding of the problem and potentially a pre-agreed mitigation.

The behaviours

The basics cover *what* you'll do on the project; the behaviours cover *how* you'll do it. In Mike's story, he was tasked with leading a group who had never worked together. They belonged to different teams, across different time zones. They also belonged to different cultures and lived different lives. The only thing connecting them was their employer. Most companies have a mission statement, supported by a set of employee values. Values like 'strive for excellence' and 'always be accountable' aren't relatable at a project level. (We made up those goals; sorry if they are the very ones adopted by your organisation!)

In recent times creating a 'team charter' has become a popular activity for new project teams. This is typically done as a workshop, where teams co-create their own set of values for the project. This sometimes coincides with naming the project. So you end up with 'Project Superman' and values like 'deliver out of this world'. To add to the theatre, sometimes workshop participants sign a 'charter' to make it legally binding that they will *deliver out of this world*. You may be able to tell from our tone that we're not huge fans of team charters. While they have a role in team building, unfortunately the project values that come out are usually no better than vacuous company-wide employee values.

There's no need to spend time dreaming up project values. If it ain't broke, don't fix it. Patrick Lencioni's '5 dysfunctions of a team' have stood the test of time as the most robust set of behaviours to monitor to ensure projects run smoothly. A recap of the five dysfunctions:

1. absence of trust (invulnerability)

2. fear of conflict (artificial harmony)

3. lack of commitment (ambiguity)

4. avoidance of accountability (low standards)

5. inattention to results (status and ego).

Repositioned as five functions of high-performing teams:

1. We trust one another.

2. We engage in unfiltered conflict around ideas.

3. We commit to decisions and plans of action.

4. We hold each other accountable for delivering against those plans of action.

5. We focus on the achievement of the collective results.

We recommend allocating 90 minutes to talk the team through these dysfunctions. Provide real-life, anonymised stories to make each one memorable. Invite discussion around them and ask if the team has experienced some of these dysfunctions. Ask the team to adhere to the five functions. Had Mike done this, he might have discovered why the team couldn't work through the backlog (number 2: artificial harmony). Instead of it being Mike's responsibility to crack the whip, the whole team would have been disturbed by the lack of progress (number 4: avoidance of accountability). Mike himself might have stopped busying himself with status reports and meetings and focused more on the team (number 5: inattention to results). We find this activity isn't good just for internal kick-off discussions but also works well with clients, or your stakeholders as a shorter meeting item (15 mins). Introduce the five dysfunctions and highlight that you'll adhere to them as a project team and ask your client or stakeholder to do so too.

Fear of conflict is all too common on new projects with external stakeholders. Most clients don't want to kick up a fuss early on in a project so they withhold any grievance, and soon a molehill becomes a mountain. It's much better to uncover a problem in week 1 rather than week 6. In summary, everyone being aware of the five dysfunctions drives the right behaviours. And you can still give your project a name if you like.

The banter

Theodore Roosevelt said, 'Nobody cares how much you know until they know how much you care.' We established in chapter 4 that it's essential to get to know the people you're working with before you start a project. This may seem bleeding obvious but in large organisations it often doesn't happen. In some instances, you might have met the people you're working with but know little about them. Teams that perform well like and trust each other. When you don't afford the time to gel with your team members, you start out of the blocks slower, as you learn one another's strengths and working styles. Clients and stakeholders can sense when a team is well formed and well acquainted rather than figuring it out on the job.

We advocate taking the time to complete a personality test as a team. It gives you an appreciation for your team members' working styles and, if you've never done one before, your own. Popular personality tests include Myers-Briggs, the Big 5 and the Insights Discovery Model. These tests are often based on Carl Jung's theory of personality types, which was based on four spectrums to define your archetype:

1. **Attitude.** Describes whether a person's attitude is directed outward (extroversion) or inward (introversion). Extroverts tend to focus on the external world and are energised by social interactions, while introverts tend to focus on their inner thoughts and feelings and need time alone to recharge.

2. **Function.** Jung identified four functions that people use to process information: thinking, feeling, sensation and intuition. These functions can be either introverted or extroverted. Introverted thinking, for example, involves analysing information internally, while extroverted thinking involves organising information in the external world.

3. **Energy.** Jung described two types of energy: extroverted and introverted. Extroverted energy is directed outward, towards the external world, while introverted energy is directed inward, towards one's inner thoughts and feelings.

4. **Lifestyle.** Jung proposed that people prefer either judging (making decisions) or perceiving (taking in information). Those who prefer judging tend to

be decisive and organised, while those who prefer perceiving tend to be flexible and spontaneous.

Our favourite is Andi Lothian's Insight Discovery Model, which translates these spectrums into four colour energies:

- **Cool Blue** (analytical thinker): Cool Blue people are analytical, logical and detail-oriented. They excel at planning, organising and following procedures. They prefer to work independently and value accuracy and precision.

- **Earth Green** (empathetic helper): Earth Green people are empathetic, nurturing and relationship-focused. They are excellent listeners and supportive team members, and value harmony and cooperation. They are often diplomatic and avoid conflict.

- **Sunshine Yellow** (energetic innovator): Sunshine Yellow people are enthusiastic, creative and spontaneous. They generate ideas, enjoy taking risks and thrive in dynamic environments. They are often persuasive communicators and enjoy collaborating with others.

- **Fiery Red** (dynamic driver): Fiery Red people are assertive, goal-oriented and decisive. They are natural leaders, take charge in situations and are driven to achieve results. They are often competitive and thrive in challenging environments.

The Insights Discovery process involves completing a questionnaire to determine an individual's colour energies. Joff was asked to take part in this process about five years into his career and wished he had done it sooner. It gave him a better appreciation for his team members' work preferences and communication style. Here are Joff's colour strengths from 2010:

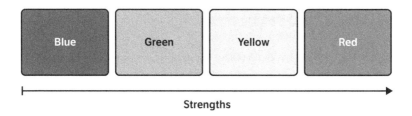

Joff used to struggle working with Cool Blues and no wonder: he was a ball of energy, keen to make decisions fast and keep excitement high. Rather than appreciating Cool Blues' analytical mindset and attention to detail, he found them slow and ponderous. It takes all types to make a great team and it's helpful to understand those types. Back in 2010, Joff's team made little Lego badges, stacked their colours and left them on their desks. It served as a useful reminder of each team member's strengths and styles. We recommend you do the same before you kick off a new project. There are heaps of free or affordable online resources and it's a great icebreaker. An hour spent getting to know one another properly is an hour that will pay dividends when the going gets tough later in the project.

Finally, and possibly most important, make time to have some fun as a team before you start a new project. Don't delay it until week one or two, because by then you'll be too busy on the project. Do something that is actually fun and completely unrelated to work. A common mistake is to try to blend the two. This is where you end up with team members holding a drink while listening to a company presentation and looking miserable. There's no need for the presentation. There will be plenty of time for work, so spend a few hours having fun. You don't need ideas from us here; do whatever your team wants to do. If there's no budget, fund it among yourselves. If some of your team are offshore, do an online quiz. Don't make excuses. Work doesn't need to be miserable. Have some fun on the company clock.

Avoid hybrid hell

Mike's CEO is considered a progressive and compassionate leader. During the pandemic he was vocally committed to supporting his workforce and the clients that Consultio served. As the world moved out of COVID lockdowns, he announced that Consultio workers would be able to work flexibly, adopting a hybrid model (from home or office) indefinitely. He announced:

'At Consultio we hire smart people and we trust them. We trust them to get their jobs done and balance their personal and professional responsibilities as they see fit. After all, I'm their CEO, not their dad.'

In 2024, as Mike and the team got ready to kick off their project, this promise remained intact. Consultio's workforce enjoy complete individual flexibility for where and how they work.

Ships in the night

When Mike kicked off the project, he thought he had a rockstar team around him to work with the offshore team members (table 5.1). His team of four was perfectly balanced to get the job done within the tight time frame and manage InsureNow's expectations.

Table 5.1: onshore team profile

Name	Skills	Role on project
Mike	Project management, stakeholder comms, budget management, agile delivery	Project Manager
Jackie	User experience and user testing	Designer
Sofia	Documenting requirements and managing user story backlog	Business Analyst
Malik	IT strategy and architecture	Technology Architect

Each team member was considered a star performer. This A-team was assembled to get the job done. Mike envisaged this would be an easy team to lead. He was wrong. Unfortunately, problems became apparent straight away. Mike initially scheduled the team's first meeting for Monday, 9 am, but Jackie declined in a note: 'Sorry, I have tennis classes every Monday and Wednesday 8.30 am – 9.30 am.' When he rescheduled for 2 pm, Sofia and Mike were at Consultio's offices, while Jackie and Malik dialled in. This wasn't seen as an issue at first. However, as the meeting unfolded Mike began writing on the whiteboard and became frustrated when Malik and Jackie couldn't see what he was writing. Malik suggested using a virtual whiteboard tool, Miro, but they all found it clunky to work in real time. Mike suggested the obvious — that they work from the office, at least for the first few weeks. The request was met with trepidation. Sofia and Malik had school pick-up every day at 3 pm, so they would need to leave by 2 pm. Jackie's husband worked in the office three days a week so she could only commit to two days in the office.

After they had discussed all their different commitments, it turned out that there was only one day a week when they could all collaborate in person. Unfortunately, this meant switching constantly between physical and digital tools.

Mike started to resent everyone else's schedules. He was a traditional 9–5 guy with an active social life outside of work. But he found that Malik and Sofia liked to log on later, once the kids were asleep, to make up their work commitments. For Mike, this meant long days waiting to review work and provide comments. As the project progressed, it became clear they weren't a team but a collection of individuals. There was little team camaraderie and while they worked together at predefined times, there was little spark. Mike did his best to keep the project on track but they couldn't keep pace with the project backlog.

Don't let your company dictate how you work

Mike's is an increasingly common tale as teams trade individual wants and needs for team performance. The outcome is that many organisations are mandating workers return to the office. At the time of writing this is on average three days a week at most large corporations. By the time you read this it may be five days, and this would be a great shame. The silver lining of the pandemic was the gift of hybrid working. We lose many hours commuting (usually spent staring at our phone). That time could be better spent on our health or with our families. If your company hasn't mandated a return to the office yet, you still have time to put up a defence. If it has, we can still help you make a compelling case to your boss that your team can deliver in a hybrid or fully remote working environment.

We have a rule in our houses. If it's not on the family planner, it's not happening. With multiple kids eight years and under, there's a lot happening, so our family planners keep us on track. Don't worry, there's not a cringe statement coming that your team is like your family. Don't create a 'family planner' with your team at work, unless you want to look goofy. However, do create a team planner.

The team planner shouldn't be overly intrusive; you don't need to know people's bedtimes, but it is helpful to know each other's social commitments. The intent here is not to be a micromanaging, overbearing project lead or boss. Quite the opposite, you're acknowledging that people have personal commitments and designing around them (within reason) to make things work. In our experience, team members find this very cathartic as they often don't want to raise personal commitments, particularly at the start of a project, and appear inflexible. This can lead to anxiety in the team member (who feels like they can't be open) and distrust within the team, if someone isn't available but hasn't shared why.

The easiest way to create your team planner is to map out a working week and ask team members to Post-it note key commitments across the working week. For Mike's team, which followed Consultio's progressive flexible working model, it might have looked something like figure 5.2.

	Monday	Tuesday	Wednesday	Thursday	Friday
Morning	**Jackie** Tennis 8:30–9:30	**Malik** Gym 8:00–9:00	**Jackie** Tennis 8:30–9:30	**Malik** Gym 8:00–9:00	
Afternoon	**Sofia & Malik** School pick-up 3:00–3:30	**Sofia & Malik** School pick-up 3:00–3:30	**Sofia & Malik** School pick-up 3:00–3:30	**Sofia & Malik** School pick-up 3:00–3:30	**Sofia & Malik** School pick-up 3:00–3:30
After work	**Mike** Soccer training	**Sofia** Zumba class	**Mike** Cinema club	**Jackie** Book club	**Weekend** All unavailable

Figure 5.2: sample team planner

Once you have a view like this, you can start to plan how you'll collaborate and perhaps compromise as a team. To enable the team to work together in person, could Sofia and Malik make other arrangements for school pick-up two days a week? People don't like being told what to do, but usually they will be prepared to compromise for the benefit of the wider team. If they could, but won't (excepting significant stress to family routine), remind them of the fifth function of successful teams — they focus on the achievement of collective results.

Lion time and tiger time

Before the pandemic it was common for project teams to be assigned a 'war room' — a room dedicated to the team for the duration of the project. Typically, these teams would end up working late hours. If you stepped into the room during the day, it would be a hub of chatter and frantic scribbling on whiteboards. If you ducked in after 6 pm, you would find the team, heads down, working away quietly. Nearly every project team that works in this manner will blame the sales team, or their boss, for these extended working hours: 'The project timeline is nuts, so we have to work longer hours.' Of course some project timelines are too tight and this puts unfair strain on the team. Sometimes, however, the team just aren't working effectively in the shared space. Joff has been in many of these war rooms and often found that the real work started later because of the recognition that they've got little done during the day. All it takes is one person to start talking about an idea and before you know it you're all back on the whiteboard. It's important that teams are deliberate in defining when they need to work together and when they need to put the headphones on and work independently.

A good way to delineate this is by distinguishing between 'lion time' and 'tiger time'. You probably don't need us to spell it out for you, but lions are social and live in a group (pride), whereas tigers are generally solitary. In a hybrid world this works perfectly as you can dictate when you need to get together to discuss ideas and when you need to work from home and work through your tasks. However, it's not just about working from home vs working in person. We've seen fully remote teams spend all day on virtual calls, allowing little tiger time to get deep work done. Lion time vs tiger time is great for restraining extroverts, who tend towards collaborative working and introverts, who might need to be persuaded to lean into team activities. It also sounds way better if, when your boss asks why the team is working from home, you can reply simply, 'It's 'tiger time'!

Don't make AI your busy accomplice

Imagine this scenario. You join a project meeting with your AI assistant (let's call this one Gen, because puns are fun) and Gen takes the minutes as the call progresses. When the meeting concludes Gen instantaneously circulates the minutes and key actions. Gen goes one step further and diarises tasks into each team member's diary. Gen follows up during the week, providing prompts for each team member to fulfil their actions, and provides a warning if any team member is falling behind. Gen proactively provides useful insights and data to help each team member with their actions. In the next meeting, Gen recaps what was discussed, prompts each team member to share their actions, takes minutes, circulates key notes ... and so it continues.

As we write this in 2024, we are on the cusp of AI becoming an integral and omnipresent tool in our teams. This scenario may be par for the course. And it sounds good, right? No-one likes being the note taker or chasing up team members for their outputs. On the surface, it might appear that Gen is helping supercharge the team's efficiency. But what if the meeting was a waste of time in the first place? What if AI was inadvertently supercharging our busy idiocy?

A tool, not a team member

It's important to remember that AI is a tool, not a team member (even though organisations like to give bots human names). And like any tool, it's only as useful as the person using it. If we train AI to be busy like us, it will likely compound our busyness. Teams should be deliberate with how they integrate AI into their workflow. The 4D framework can be useful:

- *Is it Dear?* If a task is particularly expensive, you might benefit from leveraging AI. For example, perhaps you need to translate your documents into a different language. It might be sensible to incorporate AI to help with this task rather than bringing in a contract translator.

- *Is it Dangerous?* It makes sense to use AI to undertake dangerous tasks. There are numerous uses for this in the mining and defence industries, for example.

- *Is it Dull?* This category is trickier. What is dull to one person might not be to another. We should be careful about automating work that people find rewarding, even if AI can undertake the task. The damage to overall team morale may outweigh the potential efficiency gains.

- *Can we Delete it?* Most important of all, before you automate a task, ask whether the task is even necessary. If you're not sure, delete it. You can always reinstate the task/meeting later.

Will AI cure our busyness?

As humans, we like thinking in binary terms. This is called the binary bias. It's reassuring for our brains, which struggle with lots of competing data, to dumb things down into a couple of simple options. There's evidence of this throughout society. Think politics — left wing and right wing. During the pandemic people were labelled pro-vax or anti-vax. Comic books pit Good against Evil. In the Christian religion, we learn about Heaven and Hell. The list goes on and on.

So it's no surprise that there are two competing schools of thought on the impact of AI. On the positive side, AI will cure all busywork and reduce the working day by half. AI will give us the gift of time. Companies will make more money and we'll be able to spend more time with our families. We'll even be healthier. Everyone wins. The counter-view is that AI will kill not just our busyness but also our jobs. It will displace our roles and large corporations will reap the rewards. We'll be left with no job and nothing to do, without purpose. We'll lose our way (and likely our minds). Drug addiction and crime will rise.

F. Scott Fitzgerald wrote, 'The test of a first-rate intelligence is the ability to hold two opposing views in mind at the same time and still maintain the ability to function.' Most things in life are not black or white but rather many shades of grey. AI is learning from human behaviour and data. It is also being trained to be a subservient tool (although worryingly this may change as Artificial General Intelligence (AGI) emerges). We would suggest it's more crucial than ever that we address our obsession with busyness, which is being compounded by hybrid working and our being *on* all the time. If we don't, we could end up with AI as an indefatigable busy accomplice that creates more busywork than even the most egregious boss. Use real intelligence to decide how you work and how you want to leverage AI in your teams.

Map your Team Pact

Now it's time to bring all these things together and map your Team Pact. It's helpful to complete a simple one-page document as a team before you start a project to reinforce what you're going to do and how you're going to do it. We call this mapping your Team Pact (see figure 5.3). Your Team Pact addresses three key questions that are critical to ensuring the team work productively:

1. Who is responsible for what?

2. What do we collectively believe?

3. What are we physically going to do?

How to use the Team Pact template

Make filling your Team Pact template a group activity. Print off a large A2/A1 template, or draw it on a whiteboard. Alternatively, if your team is not co-located, use a digital whiteboard tool like Miro.

What do we collectively believe?

This is the 'heart' of the project — as a team, *why* are you undertaking the project?

A: Shared behaviours

You first need to get team alignment on how you're going to work. This should be covered in the kick-off discussion leveraging

Team Pact   **Project:**......................................

Who is responsible for what?	
C. Lines of control	**D. Lines of accountability**

What do we collectively believe?	
A. Shared behaviours	**B. Shared goals**

What are we physically going to do?	
E. How we work	
F. What we need to do (scope)	**G. By when (milestones)**

Figure 5.3: the Team Pact template

the five dysfunctions of a team. A quick recap: discuss the five dysfunctions, provide anonymised, real-world examples and open to the team for discussion. If you feel strongly as a team that some of the dysfunctions don't apply to your project, feel free to amend and write your own. Individually take turns to write short statements and play back to the group for discussion. Once you have lots of statements, vote individually for your favourites and finalise your behaviours. Note that more than five becomes hard to adhere to. And heed this warning: don't be a busy idiot spending time reinventing the wheel if the five dysfunctions are fit for purpose (and in our experience they usually are).

B: Shared goals

This activity should also be covered in your well-executed kick-off discussions. You discuss and prioritise goals internally and *then* you do the same with your client or stakeholder. Don't make the mistake of thinking that you need different team goals from your client or stakeholder. Keep things simple and marry your project goals with theirs. A goal should be an outcome, not an output — for example, to improve online sales (outcome) rather than to deliver a new website (output). A reminder: if you have more than three goals, you probably have too many and you're setting the team up for failure.

Rationally, who is responsible for what?

This is the 'brain' of the project — rationally, *who* is going to make decisions?

C: Lines of control

Lines of control is a bristly topic in today's workplace, where the conversation about 'who's in charge' is often avoided. This wreaks havoc on projects. Joff has had this conversation more times than he cares to remember:

> *'I've told him several times what to do but he keeps doing it his way, which isn't right. Now we're behind schedule.'*

> *'Well, have you told him you're the Project Lead and he needs to follow your instructions?'*

> *[uncomfortable silence]*

It's always better to deal with problems early (ideally before there is a problem). Don't shy away from specifying the lines of control. Jot down who the key stakeholders are and do the same for your project team. Specify who is the key decision maker on both sides. There's no need for a power trip here. You've discussed the shared behaviours as a team, so say the following:

'As discussed, it's really important we engage in unfiltered debate around ideas. However, we do have project deadlines to stick to, so please don't be discouraged if, as the Project Lead, I give a direct instruction. It's fine if you disagree but please disagree amicably and then commit.'

You might feel uncomfortable about saying these words but trust us, you'll feel better once the words have left your mouth, and the project will run smoother as a result.

D: Lines of accountability

Lines of control should not be confused with lines of accountability. The Lead is not accountable for everything that happens on a project. Remember, the fourth function of a high-performing team is to hold each other accountable for delivering against the plans of action.

The best way to complete this section is for each team member to share what they believe their accountability is on the project and for all team members to provide feedback. The Project Lead ultimately signs off these lines of accountability. This is a really important step. Like lines of control, often teams shy away from individual accountability. This leads to the inevitable 'I thought you were doing that', and causes mistrust and friction. Agree up front on lines of accountability.

What are we physically going to do?

This is the 'body' of the project — *how* and *what* are we going to do as a team?

E: How we work

Here you distil your shared calendar into bite-size form. This might be as simple as writing the times allocated for lion time and tiger time. If you're running an agile project, this might be the place you add in your sprint plan (daily standups, retros, showcases). It should not replicate all the detail in your project plan but should give a snapshot of the key weekly meetings for your project team.

F: What we need to do (scope)

It's important as a project team that you don't lose sight of what you actually have committed to delivering. Write those deliverables here …

G: By when (milestones)

… and specify the milestones for each one. Project plans can have lots of moving parts, so it's helpful to have a snapshot of *what* you need to deliver and *when*.

Figure 5.4 shows an example of a completed Team Pact template.

Team Pact

Project: InsureNow site

Who is responsible for what?

C. Lines of control

Sponsor: InsureNow Head of marketing
Team Project Lead: Mike

D. Lines of accountability

Mike: Overall Project Lead
Jackie: Designer (UI)
Sofia: Business Analyst (documenting requirements)
Malik: Tech Architect (integration and testing plans)

What do we collectively believe?

A. Shared behaviours
1. We trust one another
2. We engage in unfiltered conflict around ideas
3. We commit to decisions and plans of action
4. We hold each other accountable for delivering against those plans of action
5. We focus on the achievement of the collective results.

B. Shared goals
1. New revenue growth
2. Improve brand positioning
3. Protect market share from competitors and new market entrants.

What are we physically going to do?

E. How we work

Tues, Wed: Lion time
Mon, Thurs: Tiger time
Friday, 9am: Project status meeting (internal)
Friday 12pm: Project status meeting (external)

F. What we need to do (scope)

Design concept ⟶ By week 4 (May 10th)

MVP ⟶ Week 12 (July 8th)

Final go-live ⟶ Week 24 (September 27th)

G. By when (milestones)

Figure 5.4: example of a completed Team Pact template

Lead by example

Leadership appointments can sometimes feel unjustified or downright unfair. That's life — it happens. Make peace with the fact that the world isn't always fair. If you follow the steps in creating your Team Pact, you can still ensure you're productive and successful, even if your leader is underperforming. Remember, leadership is earned, not appointed. Leadership and influence are often confused. Even if you're not the Manager/Leader, you can still recommend the techniques in this chapter for your project teams. Imagine you're an up-and-coming football player, you're 19 and paid a pittance. Meanwhile, the star striker is a seasoned international who is paid millions of dollars. One day you're called off the bench and thrust onto the pitch. What do you do? Try to score a goal to prove you're ready for the starting line-up (and a better contract) or refuse to go on? Your professional career is like that, except you have the added benefit that you don't actually have to wait for the coach to tap you on the shoulder. The best way to get a promotion is first to prove you can do the job.

Being a successful leader is more than having this toolkit to help with team productivity (although it certainly helps build trust and successful teams). Joff has had 19 bosses over his past two decades of working, not including all his indirect superiors. When you work for organisations with hundreds of thousands of employees, that's a lot of bosses. Over the years, we've learned what good leadership looks like and what ineffective leadership looks like. We've been in many meetings where 'the boss' isn't actually the person everyone is listening to. We remember these people and watch their careers take off, and when the boss moves on/out, they are usually the heir apparent. Practise leadership before you become a leader. Following are five traits you should keep close and work on to become a good leader.

1. Judgement

Strategy is often misunderstood. Richard Rumelt, in his excellent book *The Crux*, provides a simple definition: 'strategy is a considered judgement about what to do'. Judgement, we would argue, is the most important leadership trait. In our experience, it is also the hardest to teach. How can you know what's happening in someone's gut? How can you make better decisions?

As humans, we've never been great at processing large amounts of data on which to make rational decisions. Herbert Simon, who won a Nobel Prize in Economics in 1978 for his theory on bounded rationality, coined the term 'satisficing' (combining the verbs *satisfy* and *suffice*). The theory proposed that the rationality of individuals is limited by the information they have, the cognitive limitations of their minds and the finite amount of time they have to make decisions. Simon argues, therefore, that we all make decisions that are 'good enough', rather than optimal. Artificial intelligence is helping us to distil data and determine the best course of action. Real human intelligence, however, will still be needed to make judgement calls. Humans also do things that sometimes don't make sense and there can be beauty (and major financial gains) in this irrationality. So how do you improve your judgement?

Experience undoubtedly helps, providing you learn from it. This requires effort and humility. It's easy, when something doesn't go the way you want it to, to blame external forces beyond your control. It's mentally reassuring to park an issue, determine 'it wasn't my fault' and move on. When leaders do this they damage not only their own propensity to learn and improve but also the wider team's. For example, when company *x* loses a customer, the CEO announces to the team, 'We did an amazing job. It wasn't our fault — the customer got it wrong.' This isn't helpful. There may be some truth in it, but a better reaction is to focus on how you can improve. This is not about assigning blame; it's about making the effort to reflect on what you could do differently next time. If you're leading a project, it's best to do this in the immediate aftermath of the project. We like the term 'hotwash', stolen from the air force, who clean their planes soon after they land as it's easier to get the dirt off while the planes are still hot. Schedule a project hotwash in your project plan at the start of the project, it's all too easy to move on to the next thing once the project is finished.

There are many frameworks for running a project retrospective, but we like 'the four Ls'. Grab some sharpies and Post-it notes and ask each team member to reflect on the following four questions individually, share back (one thought per Post-it note) then synthesise the data to get to some key insights:

- *Loved.* What did you love about the project?

- *Loathed.* What did you loathe about the project?

- *Lacked.* What did you lack on the project?

- *Longed for.* What did you long for on the project?

If you're not running a project and reflecting on day-to-day business operations or team performance, you might ask:

- What should we start doing?

- What should we stop doing?

- What should we continue doing?

Learned experience is not the only factor that improves judgement. Plenty of leaders have shown bad judgement, and chapter 3 offers tips on how to thrive under a busy idiot boss. Regardless of your level of experience, you can work on your clarity of thought to make better judgement calls. Think deeply about your most important priority, a challenge you can solve, as it's foolhardy to pick something that's not within your control. When you're making a decision ask yourself these questions:

- Will this course of action help me achieve my most important priority?

- Is the timing right to take this course of action now?

- Do I have the time to invest in completing this task properly?

If it's a big decision with broad implications for the team or business, ask:

- Should I get someone else's opinion before I make this decision?

Let's take a simple example. Imagine you run a coffee shop and your key priority for the year is to improve food sales. Someone approaches you about selling their collection of giftware in your shop. Is that going to help you improve food sales? Are you willing to take the time to set up a small retail space and start advertising that you sell giftware? Good judgement is not just about deciding what you should do but also about showing restraint towards all those things you shouldn't. Restraint is a grossly undervalued leadership skill. Great leaders, we're told, 'lead from the front' and 'make bold decisions'. But doing nothing may sometimes be the best judgement call.

Behind every busy idiot is bad judgement. You will make bad decisions and at times act like a busy idiot. If you catch yourself, however, you can ensure this doesn't become your default.

Improve your judgement by learning from your experience and thinking deeply about your priority goals before making a decision and taking a course of action.

2. Communication

A common mistake is to assume communication is synonymous with talking. In fact, it's quite the opposite. The best communicators are good listeners. While there are lots of books, TED talks and courses on how to become a great speaker, the same can't be said about developing good listening skills. We're talking here about properly listening, often called 'active listening'. Many people pretend to be listening but they're actually just waiting to speak. This is particularly common in sales meetings, where the salesperson is so eager to sell that they forget to ask what the customer wants to buy. There's security in dominating the conversation, but it makes for a very disengaging experience. The same can be said of when you're speaking to a direct report, if you jump straight to solutions and talk more than they do, the chances that you'll miss the mark are high. Most of the time, it's not about providing a solution but about giving your direct report space to share their thoughts and feedback. So how, practically, do you become a better listener?

First, change your mindset when you go into meetings. Think about questions, not pre-baked answers. A simple question to ask a direct report is, 'What's on your mind?' The next best question is, 'What else?' If they raise an issue, before jumping on your soapbox to show how smart you are, ask, 'I've got a view on this but before I share it, what do *you* think?' By taking time to ask questions and actively listen, you build your understanding and connection with the person you're speaking with. You build trust. It's not easy. Most people find it more tiring to listen and truly focus on what's being said than to wax lyrical. It also requires humility and confidence in equal doses. Humility, as you start a conversation based on the understanding that you don't have all the answers. Also, confidence as you enter a conversation knowing that you can roll with the punches, whichever direction the conversation takes. A good rule of thumb: if you're in a meeting with a direct report and you're doing most of the talking, you're not listening hard enough. Better that you spend 70 to 80 per cent of the time listening. A 1v1 conversation with a direct report is their meeting, not yours, so give them the time to tell you what's on their mind.

When you're not in a conversation but communicating top-down to a team, it's wise to remember this line from George Lakoff's book *The Metaphors We Live By*: 'put thought into words as if they were shopping bags'. Just as shopping bags carry groceries, your words carry ideas, meaning and intent. If you don't think carefully about the words you use when speaking to your team, your message might be misconstrued. You might have great judgement, but it will count for little if you can't articulately share your plan. If you can't communicate effectively, you won't be able to take your team on the journey, and if you don't have a team you're no longer a leader. Many problems arise from poor communication. Molehills become mountains as a result of a few misplaced words and it takes time to repair trust and confidence with the team. You've seen some examples of this in this book! Think straight, talk straight is useful in helping you be more deliberate and effective with your communication. Communicating effectively builds confidence in your abilities. The more confidence people have in you, the more autonomy you'll have generally. Autonomy is a great antidote to being a busy idiot!

A final note on communication. As we have noted, there are plenty of resources on public speaking, and to do the subject justice would require its own book. One thing is certain, though: practice makes perfect. Also, don't believe anyone who says they love public speaking (we have said this in the past to try to convince ourselves!). As with everything in life, the more you do it, the easier it becomes. So when you are asked to speak publicly, even if it makes you feel sick in your stomach and you have an alibi, say yes. The fact that something is hard is just one more reason to do it. You'll emerge a better communicator and a more confident human being.

3. Inspiration

If you want to lead, you have to inspire. There are two tenets to inspiration: curiosity and confidence.

Curiosity

In his book *The Hard Thing about the Hard Things*, Ben Harrowitz describes leadership as 'getting someone to follow you, even if only out of curiosity'. The best way to instil curiosity is to stay curious yourself. First, commit to life-long learning. This means different things to different people. If you're academically inclined, you might continue to collect new certifications and academic honours. If you're like us, it just means you read, or listen to audiobooks or podcasts, every day. It amazes us when we hear people say they don't have time to read. Yet, everyone seems to have time to watch TV. You don't even have to choose between the two. We have young kids and busy jobs and we do both. Learning is a habit and it's one you have to create if you want to form new ideas and stay curious. Joff, in an attempt to make a mockery of the first chapter of this book, uses the Kindle app on his phone. For him, this means whenever he's in transit, or has some downtime between meetings, he opens the app and reads. For others, doing the exact opposite works better: they buy a print book to avoid the distracting lure of their phone. James Clear, in his bestseller *Atomic Habits*, does a great job of explaining how you can stack actions to form habits. For example, when I do *x*, I always do *y*. For reading, this might be 'whenever I'm on the train, I always read'.

The second aspect to curiosity is adopting an experimentation mindset. When you have new ideas, you need to test them in a smart way that doesn't cause too much disruption if the idea turns out to be misguided. When testing a new idea, ask yourself these guiding questions:

- How do I test this idea quickly at low cost and with limited effort?

- What does success look like? How will I measure it?

- What's the right time frame for this experiment?

By adopting this mindset, you'll be able to innovate and keep the team curious as you try new things, without creating lots of disturbance and breaking trust with big-bang failures.

Confidence

Confidence needs a fine balance. Too much and you become arrogant and complacent; too little and you'll come across as meek and unsure. The sweet spot is to be confident but modest. When you decide on a course of action, go forward with conviction, even though you know you may be wrong. Telling yourself that you may be wrong is not about introducing doubt and eroding your confidence. Quite the opposite. Business is complex and there's often no simple answer. Knowing you may be wrong gives you permission to move forward with confidence.

The other way to build confidence is to hire the best people. Success is easier when you surround yourself with successful people. This may seem obvious but we've seen leaders shy away from hiring people who have more experience or better qualifications. Don't be intimidated by hiring people you think might be smarter than you. The job of the leader is to build the best possible team. You'll feel confident having an A-team in your corner.

The true test of these two tenets is when things go bad. Can you still instil curiosity and confidence in the team when things aren't going as well as you'd hoped? For this, you'll need to practise resilience and candour. You may feel terrible about a downturn in the market or some bad business results. But you're the leader. You can't blame your boss or present yourself as defeated and seek sympathy. You've got to show up and stand tall.

4. Empathy

Empathy may be the most important and underrated leadership trait. Remember, 'nobody cares how much you know until they know how much you care'. Leadership is earned by trust. You build trust when you take the time to truly invest in your team and their success and not just your own. Everybody has their own problems and those problems might not always be visible. Treat people as you would wish to be treated, with kindness. Use the communication tips listed earlier to actively listen to your individual team members' hopes, dreams and fears. Leaders who do this have lower attrition rates and don't have to spend as much time trying to recruit new team members. Leading with empathy fosters a team culture in which team members feel confident in speaking out and sharing ideas. You'll be able to innovate better and respond to customer demands better. By leading empathetically, you'll make better decisions because you'll have a deeper understanding of a wide range of thoughts and perspectives.

Leading with empathy is beneficial not just for employee satisfaction, but also for customers. Businessolver, in their *2023 State of Workplace Empathy Report*, indicated that organisations with empathetic leadership have 17 per cent higher profits compared to those without. Modern corporations have become obsessed with data, but this usually refers to analytics and quantitative data. To build empathy with your customers, you need to conduct qualitative research. This involves speaking to your customers in their context when they interact with your products and services. Quantitative data gives you a clue to what the issues are, but you can't build empathy from stats. Qualitative data unravels what's going on. Designing with customers for customers is the only way to gain empathy and improve customer advocacy for your business. Think of the Japanese expression, *Genchu Gembutsu*, which originated from Zen Buddhist teaching and can be translated as 'go see for yourself'. It has been adopted as a principle of 'the Toyota Way', a management philosophy that emphasises continuous improvement, respect for people and standardisation to achieve efficiency, quality and customer satisfaction. If you're struggling to build empathy with your employees or customers, stop gazing at spreadsheets and go see for yourself.

As a leader, you'll sometimes have to make tough business decisions. Redundancies, for example, are never kind. In these situations, don't hide behind your corporate shield and business-speak. This happens too often. Filtered through HR and legal departments, emails like the following are scripted: 'Due to unforeseen economic headwinds, we have started a cost optimisation plan, which will help streamline our resources and better equip the business to execute on its growth ambitions and our commitment to customers and shareholders. If you are receiving this email, unfortunately your role in the business has been made redundant…' Language like this is dehumanising and paves the way for cynicism or apathetic behaviour. When large corporations call their employees 'resources' they are inferring that they are a tool to be used up and replaced. When you have to make tough decisions, speak in plain English. Don't fall into the habit of thinking you're an important executive and not a human being first. That's what busy idiots do.

5. Consistency

Who you are is what you do most of the time, not what you do some of the time; in the words of James Clear, 'you get what you repeat'. Busy idiots don't think deeply about what they're doing each day so their priorities change with every meeting they attend. They are lost and grabbing answers wherever they can find them. They start initiatives based on a whim, forget about them and move on to the next ill-conceived plan. In time, some employees working under a busy idiot boss learn to take what they say with a pinch of salt and disengage. Others desperately try to keep up with their boss's changing expectations and end up burnt out, frustrated and upset.

So how do you work on consistency? First, do what you say you're going to do. Nothing breaks trust quicker than a broken promise. This means you have to be careful about what you say yes to (refresh your memory about this in chapter 5 if you need to) so you can keep a high say/do ratio. Second, stay committed to your priorities and be consistent about how you communicate them to the team. For example, imagine you're a supermarket executive and you tell your team that the number one priority is providing customers with the lowest prices. A month later, you start asking questions about the range of products and demand answers on how the range can be improved. A month later still you ask questions about the in-store experience and what new technology should be introduced.

All of these areas would be important to a supermarket executive, but goals need to be prioritised and the hierarchy needs to be clearly communicated. The question regarding in-store experience would be better asked as, 'Are there ways to improve our in-store experience that won't impact our priority goal of giving customers the lowest prices?' When you stick to the script, you empower your team to execute the strategy. They know what you're thinking. If you change your mind after every meeting, you're on your way to being a busy idiot and the team will be hamstrung and dependent on you consistently communicating what you want.

This doesn't of course mean you can't change your mind. It's critical that every leader should be prepared to change her/his mind in light of new data or circumstances. But you need to give your strategy a chance to succeed, or fail. When it comes to your most critical business challenge, 18 months is a good yardstick. As we've discussed, you can experiment around the edges but your team needs to know what the rallying cry is so they can get on with their jobs without you creating a bottleneck.

A final word on consistency. Leaders whose temperament and concerns change like the wind wreak havoc with their team's emotions. As an employee, it's hard to be productive when you don't know which version of your boss is going to turn up each day. Lead with a calm demeanour. There will be times when you're frustrated, maybe even angry, but you're the leader so suck it up. Take a deep breath and be calm. If you struggle to maintain your cool, fear not. In the next chapter we'll talk about how you can work on your mindfulness.

You can't go it alone: how to form productive teams

1. **Start as you mean to go on**

   When team building, apply the 3B framework:

   - *Basics*. Discuss and prioritise your project goals as a team.

   - *Behaviours*. Familiarise your team with Lencioni's five dysfunctions.

   - *Banter*. Make the time to get to know each other.

    Top tip: Work doesn't have to be miserable—have some fun on the company clock!

2. **Avoid hybrid hell**

   - Acknowledge that we all have busy lives and create a team planner.

   - Schedule lion and tiger time on projects.

    Top tip: Don't let your boss dictate how you work—find your own rhythm!

3. Don't make AI your busy accomplice

- Use the 4D framework (is it dear, dangerous, dull or deletable?) to determine how you integrate AI into your workflows.

 Top tip: Remember that AI is a tool, not a team member.

4. Map your Team Pact

Remember the three questions that are critical to helping your team work productively:

- Who is responsible for what?

- What do we collectively believe?

- What are we physically going to do?

 Top tip: Print a copy of your Team Pact and stick it on your study/office wall.

5. Lead by example

Reflect on the four traits of good leadership:

- *Judgement.* Learn from your mistakes and practise your clarity of thought.

- *Communication.* The best communicators are active listeners.

- *Inspiration.* Remember the two key tenets, curiosity and confidence.

- *Empathy.* You can't build empathy from stats. Think *Genchu Gembutsu* — go see for yourself!

 Top tip: Don't fall into the habit of thinking you're an important executive and not a human being first.

CHAPTER 6

Family life: work to live or live to work— it's your call

By this point you are a master of managing your tech, your time and your team. Let's now turn our attention to how this can help you live a happier and more fulfilling life outside of work. We'll also cover how to make sure your busy boss or busy team doesn't intrude on your home and family life. This chapter is all about our *sustainable grounding*: now we spend less time being a busy idiot, how do we get back to living life?

Juggling priorities

Chris is a high achiever. He played college basketball while managing top marks to gain entry to postgrad law school where he went on to achieve an MBA and Juris Doctorate in Law. After graduation he landed a legal position at a tech company in Silicon Valley, where he and his wife Courtney moved to settle into their careers. Courtney is a high-level IT engineer, so a move to California and access to top companies was an easy decision for them. Both found companies that offered unlimited leave, which appealed to their travel bug and was a perk both felt was too good to pass up!

Chris made a flying start at his new role! He often worked 10-hour days, but he was no stranger to hard work. After all, the legal profession has a culture of long hours, so Chris rationalised that he would likely be working more hours if he was in a traditional law firm. He was a go-getter and helped his tech company increase their global footprint, and ultimately see growth only heard of in the most successful tech companies. As the company grew, the boundary between Chris's work hours and his life outside of work became increasingly blurred. International growth came with video conferencing meetings on London and Hong Kong time.

This was stressful but manageable for the young couple, who were each supportive of the other's career. At times they would miss dinner or planned events with family and friends, but then many of their friends faced the same work challenges they did.

Fast-forward a few years, and Chris and Courtney have a young family: two kids and a dog. Their mornings start at 6 with the kids awake and active. By 7 they are tag teaming, with one getting dressed as the other prepares breakfast. While serving breakfast Chris is on his phone as messages from London (where it is mid-afternoon) demand his immediate action on a legal 'nightmare'. Chris paces the kitchen and responds to his phone, while one child feeds the dog his breakfast under the table. Courtney comes out to 'switch' and opens her laptop to check emails as per her morning ritual. She sees the unread emails creeping over the 2000 mark and frantically tries to clear some to get it to a more 'controllable' backlog. Chris comes back out on a work call, with one earbud in, on mute and video off, he tries his level best to tune into the latest crisis from the London office, but it's difficult with kids running around as he attempts to dress them for daycare.

By 8 Chris wrangles the kids into the car to drop them at daycare before heading for the office. He lets out a deep breath before realising in the chaos of the morning that he forgot to eat breakfast, left his coffee at home and is wearing mismatching business shoes (one brown, one black). Courtney is working from home. She takes a minute to reset but has one eye on the kitchen counter where her email inbox continues to tick over.

Chris spends his 9–5 in meeting after meeting, most of which are on Zoom. He comes out of those meetings with an efficient list of action items, which he reviews that evening after the kids are in bed.

Chris and Courtney can't wait for their family holiday. After all, one of the perks of their jobs was the unlimited leave! They book a family vacation in Hawaii. It's amazing, it gives them time for family activities and the kids are having a blast. But there's something wrong. That unlimited leave that looked so enticing on paper hasn't worked out as they had hoped. Chris's company has gone through rapid growth and as a result is under-resourced. There's simply no-one to take over his role while he's in Hawaii, which means sporadic work calls. It's not the 10-hour days he routinely puts in, but a more manageable two to three hours. It still looks good on paper — idyllic white sand beaches and 70 per cent less work! So why doesn't Chris feel relaxed? Courtney feels less pressure to attend video meetings, but that inbox keeps on growing, and she dreads letting it creep up while on leave. She knows she will spend the first month back working overtime to clear her inbox.

So what went wrong?

It's not Chris and Courtney's fault. Welcome to the modern workplace, where the lines between family and work life are frequently fuzzy. Blurring these boundaries has profound impacts on our wellbeing and mental health. There are very few people in this world who can operate in that way for a sustained period of time. In this chapter, we'll take you through how to 'un-blur' them, and help you regain a sense of control at home.

Your home is your castle

Any Australian will know immediately where we are going with this. In 1997, the iconic Aussie film *The Castle* hit the cinemas. For international readers unfamiliar with the movie, it's a comedy based on the working-class Kerrigan family and their fight to save their home from being acquired by the international airport expansion project next door. Darryl Kerrigan (the father), giving evidence in court, famously declares, 'It's not a house, it's a home. A man's home is his castle!' Simply put, in Darryl's mind, in your house you're the boss. Perhaps that was truer in the 1990s, but we might question if it's still the case today. Do you feel your home is your castle? Does it still provide the sanctuary from work, school, and outside noise and pressure that you and your family badly need?

Chris and Courtney definitely don't feel it. Their workplace culture and teams have contributed to busyness at home and their slipping into busy idiot habits at home. But what does 'home' mean these days? With so many of us doing WFH and hybrid working the word doesn't refer to a physical space anymore. But we should be clear. We're not suggesting all modern workplaces operate like Chris's and Courtney's. Let's assume they are extreme (but not uncommon) examples. You might read their story and see a few elements you can identify with in your current work environment, but for the purposes of this exercise we'll run with their example. If it doesn't apply to your current workplace, think of it as a laundry list of red flags for any future organisations you consider joining.

Build your castle: how to be more present at home

To be present at home and get the downtime you need to counter illness, stress, burnout and a host of other established side effects, let's take a look at the key ways in which work stress can 'leak' into your home life, primarily aided by technology designed to make your job and life 'easier'.

Here are the eight steps to building your castle:

1. Sustainable audit and harvest

We did a deep dive into this in chapter 2, and for good reason. The first step to building your castle is to use the audit tools and harvest trees to establish a solid platform. Once you've done that we can look at the following steps that touch on some specific areas of concern at home, socially and in your family life.

2. If possible, build a moat around your castle

We have established the benefits of face-to-face work, specifically around improving neural pathways, optimising oxytocin and combating loneliness. If you have the luxury of living within an easy commute of the office, then we advise you spend as much of your 'working hours' as you can there. The routine of waking up, getting dressed, commuting, stopping by your favourite coffee shop on the way, and so on may sound boring but it has incredible health and psychological benefits. We humans crave social interaction and routine. The physical separation between work and home life can also serve as a psychological marker between the two. With some self-discipline, the commute can be your cue to transition from one to the other.

It's the most straightforward strategy to build a moat around your castle and be more present at home. The most literal example of moat building would be to leave all your work devices at the office. A pretty radical suggestion, we know. But if you regularly work from the office, and you don't intend to let work spill into your home life, it's the ultimate pre-commitment contract with yourself to ensure discipline.

For those working in a fantastic global organisation that spares you from a long commute or even allows you to work in a different city or country from your company, building a moat is slightly more complicated but not impossible. You could, for example, maintain a physical work/life separation by designating a specific space in your house as the only place you can work. Don't blur the boundaries by bringing family/leisure inside or working outside of that home office. Imagine a moat across that doorway.

Brad does WFH half the week and had a designated office in his house, but failed to maintain the separation. There was always a temptation to run and grab some food, which led to taking the kitchen rubbish out, then noting the height of the weeds in the front yard … and so it went on, and before he knew it there was an hour lost. The solution for Brad was to build a small office pod in the garden. Not the most financially friendly and realistic solution for most, but it successfully created enough physical separation to encourage deep and focused periods of undistracted work.

If you have a home office space, but are sometimes tempted to creep in just to quickly check your email, to see if that big proposal has come through, consider hanging an 'out of office' sign on the door as a visual reminder, or for more dramatic effect put a lock on the door, thereby creating even more friction!

Some incredibly progressive organisations have started to take this concept to the next level by introducing times of the day (such as 7 pm to 7 am) when the email servers and messaging platforms are down. It's a brilliant concept that would be best done in consultation with each team, establishing agreement around what hours would work best for the servers to be offline.

3. Downtime

What are your favourite activities to help you unwind and relax? It may be reading, watching a fantastic show with your partner, cooking or pursuing a home-friendly hobby. When was the last time you did that without your phone or other technology breaking your flow of relaxation?

We have ground-breaking information for you: despite our steady march towards AI we are *not* cyborgs. Humans need to unwind and relax, even if it takes the form of watching another predictable episode of *Ramsay's Kitchen Nightmares*. But our Zen-like activities are usually interrupted with a ping from a work email or a notification from the kids' soccer group chat. We have already outlined persuasive design and our autopilot response that is very difficult to combat.

Just as you manage your work calendar, you need to manage your downtime calendar to protect you from unnecessary interruption. If you enjoy cooking and listening to music in the kitchen, that 20 minutes of the day is precious for your mental health. You get none of the benefits if you cave to the soccer group chat about having the correct club socks for the game in three weeks' time. In fact, your downtime morphs into a background activity while you try to recall what day the club uniform shop is open. Then you search the family calendar on your phone to see if your partner has a window this weekend to resolve this urgent crisis. The end result? Busy idiot cooking and you've served up a meal on the family dining table and can't recall what ingredients you used.

This scenario also plays out with work-related pings. Watching your favourite sport on TV (a cliché, we know, but the ultimate downtime for these two authors) at 8 pm on a weeknight, you have innocently placed your phone on the coffee table. It pings, and of course we go down the persuasive design rabbit hole and read it automatically like a good busy idiot. We tell ourselves, 'It's just one email. I'll just see what they want and flag it for tomorrow.' Ten minutes later the score has changed multiple times but we have no idea what happened as most of our cognitive processing has focused on that work email.

We need to accept that most of us are no match for our technology's persuasive design and that finding ways to leave our devices in a different room or to reduce their alerts and notifications is key. If this is you, revisit 'Sustainable harvest' in chapter 2.

4. Mindfulness

What a fantastic concept! Many of you will be familiar with it since it took the corporate world by storm around ten years ago. Suddenly all the staff wellbeing programs referred to mindfulness, and there were all manner of mindful corporate retreats: forest bathing, forest walking, forest stick throwing — okay, we made the last one up. Our issue with mindfulness is not with the theory or empirical evidence of its relieving stress, which is genuinely solid. Our issue is the way it overcomplicates things.

So our definition of mindfulness is simply doing any activity while giving it your full and undivided attention. To break it down further, think of activities that require you to use your five senses: sight, touch, sound, taste, smell. We would argue that if you are using even a few of them consciously in any activity you are doing it mindfully.

Brad recently ran a workshop at a leading international consulting firm with an incredibly intelligent and successful group of participants. After the session a man in his late twenties approached Brad looking like he had a lightbulb moment to share. He described the favourite part of his day as walking his dog each morning on the local beach. But this guy had slowly found his way to becoming a busy idiot. What started out as listening to his favourite music streaming platform on his walk transitioned into checking his social media. A few months later, he explained, he started telling himself, 'I'll just check what's on today' by looking at his calendar, followed by doomscrolling and even checking work emails. His mindful morning beach walk had become a stress-inducing nightmare.

We joked about his predicament, and possible solutions, including using a stripped-back smartwatch instead of his phone, before he declared, 'I don't need the music. I want to walk on the beach and listen to the sounds around me! And be available to say hello and chat to other dog walkers.' Social connection. Oxytocin. Brilliant.

5. Meals

Full disclosure, we both grew up with what can only be described as 'very British' fathers. Dinner and most mealtimes were had at the dining room table and you didn't leave until everyone was finished. We understand that's not everyone's cultural norm, and that's okay, but in most cultures meals are a time of social connection and sharing. We are sure many of you would agree that this tradition has been eroding over the past decade as devices disrupt long-held custom. It's easy for us to blame young people and teenagers, and we'll get into that soon, but most adults are guilty of this as well.

Simple solutions we like include a blanket no phones at the table policy, but sometimes this rule is too easy to breach when we are stressed and tired. If that's you, consider trying what we call a table safe — a box that sits proudly in the middle of the table into which all phones are placed at the start of the meal. If you want to step it up a notch, you can add a lock on the box for dramatic effect.

6. Connecting with friends

This is a logical one to tackle next, as many of our most prized connections occur while sharing a meal or a drink with friends. Next time you are out on a work lunch or having coffee with friends try this little experiment. Challenge your friends to a friendly wager. Suggest that all of you put your phones on the table (face down) and the first person to touch their phone (consciously or on autopilot) must pay for the table's drinks. Even if there is a poor busy idiot who lasts only a few minutes, it establishes a social norm within the group that you value one another's company and attention.

7. Sleep

Healthy sleep patterns may be the single biggest casualty of busy idiot behaviour. Poor sleep has a profound impact on our health. There's no magic formula for good sleep, but most of us require about eight hours a night and benefit from a regular sleep routine and what experts refer to as good 'sleep hygiene', meaning behaviours and habits to manage a healthy routine around sleep.

Let's revisit our friends Chris and Courtney. When your workplace encourages busy idiot behaviour, and you are obliging, it's difficult to see a scenario where sleep is not impacted. Chris may have planned to get his eight hours' sleep between 10 pm and 6 am. That would require him to start his routine around 9 pm each night, starting with a shower, a cup of tea and reading in bed. But what if between 8 and 9 pm Chris is working solidly to action all the items arising from the day's meetings and this runs overtime.

Or, perhaps worse, what if a young co-worker has decided to shift her flexible work hours to later at night as she has no kids and that better fits her lifestyle. In chapter 5, we shared some practical tips on how to work as one cohesive team, regardless of your company's working models. In this scenario, Chris's 'focus overtime' period means a stream of emails floods his inbox around 8.30 pm. Chris's stress levels surge as he ruminates, 'I'm already behind. Tomorrow morning will be a nightmare if I don't clear these out.' The stress boosts Chris's cortisol levels. Our friend cortisol is linked with sleep disturbance and insomnia. Chris begins his sleep routine late and finds himself staring at the ceiling at midnight, telling himself, 'I'm going to be a wreck tomorrow.' Sleep is sacred. When it is seriously disturbed, we are usually heading into a vicious cycle that can be difficult to break.

8. Exercise

Whether you run ultra-marathons or enjoy a game of badminton, what matters is that you maintain a healthy exercise routine to support your physical and mental health. Trap number one to watch out for is exercise being usurped by the work deadline in front of you. That's classic busy idiot behaviour. It's a nil sum game. You skip the morning walk, rationalising that it will give you an extra 40 minutes to tackle that proposal due today. But by doing so you deprive yourself of the serotonin (another feel-good neurochemical) that would have lifted your mood, energy and concentration. That shot of serotonin makes you more productive, so skipping your exercise routine to make more time for work is a flawed trade-off.

Trap number two with exercise is related to mindfulness. While providing physical health benefits, exercise also provides psychological benefits, many of which are delivered through the practice of doing that activity in a mindful way.

We've already observed how mindfulness doesn't have to be a complicated practice. Take running, for instance. Most of us have given it a crack at some point in our lives. Running practically forces you to be mindful by tuning in to your five senses. Your focus and attention are on your steps, the obstacles you are avoiding, the sounds you hear and your breathing. But if you let work or social tech invade your exercise (checking that message or stopping to take a phone call) it becomes a lot less mindful.

How to quell the uprising: kids and technology

If you are a parent, grandparent, even aunt or uncle, and have little ones in your life, this is likely a concern that has been on your radar. It's not a primary focus of this book, but it can certainly contribute to our stress levels, hence it can play a role in causing busy idiot behaviour. At the end of the day, if you have spent a good portion of the day arguing with your kids as you attempt to police their screen time, then it's a significant stressor in your life. If you have woken up in the night to discover your tween commando crawling across the lounge room to 'steal back' their phone, which was placed on charge, then 'significant stressor' probably barely covers it.

This is an area we are both very conscious of and struggle to navigate. Brad recently presented at a global organisation where hundreds of concerned parents gave up an hour of their time (for many, their lunch break) to tune in. In the post-session feedback survey one of the attendees wrote, 'This should be compulsory learning for humanity at all levels … as we navigate such an acceleration in technology proliferation within our lifestyle and the ubiquity of its reach.' Poignant words! But what surprised us most was that attendee's job title, which was in the digital/IT space. The assumption that if we had more tech skills we could 'solve' the problem just doesn't stack up when even cyber experts struggle at home.

The impact of tech on a developing brain

In chapter 1, we reviewed the persuasive design elements common to social media, gaming and all forms of tech that our kids have access to. We also established that most of the software apps and tools are fairly easy to get around, cannon fodder for a 13-year-old who can simply visit Google or YouTube for easy tutorials on how to get around parental controls.

Just what impact technology and constant screen use have on us psychologically, developmentally and neurologically has become somewhat clearer over the past ten years, although there are still significant mixed messages out there for parents. All we will say is that most of the bona fide health and medical research in this field point to clear impacts on children. The contention usually (not always) comes from academics and researchers in the fields of computer science, communication, game design ... you get the point. When they hear 'Professor Y' or 'Dr Z' claiming there's no evidence of screen use negatively impacting our children, it's easy for busy parents to trust these conclusions while ignoring the counterarguments.

We know excessive screen use has neurological impacts on the developing brain. Functional MRI (fMRI) longitudinal studies show evidence of cognitive decline in kids who use screens for three to five hours a day, and neurological evidence of the brain cortex thinning prematurely with more than seven hours' use a day (Paulus et al. 2019).

A common argument is that we live in a digital world and kids need to learn how to self-regulate their screen use. This argument is flawed at best and laughable at worst. The areas of the brain responsible for emotional and impulse control (the prefrontal cortex) don't fully develop until around age 21 in women and the late twenties in men (some research suggests even later!). The idea that little Sally can manage her own phone use at age 8, 12 or even 15 is silly. Not that we are suggesting that no children can manage their screen use responsibly; we're just talking about the average tween or teen. Handing them unfettered access to screens without boundaries is comparable to handing a 12-year-old the keys to the family car and a six-pack of beer and telling them they need to 'learn how to self-regulate'.

Many countries are seeing a groundswell of support for limits on children's screen time through banning phones in schools and lifting age limits to access social media. Will these changes work? Not sure. It's a complicated problem, but it's an encouraging sign that parents and society as a whole are beginning to recognise the risks for our children and teenagers.

What should I do?

There are steps you can take to limit your kids' screen time without causing a full-blown war in your house and ongoing stress to you as a parent. Best established in the early years (age 5–10), they can be implemented later if you missed the boat.

For more on this, check out Brad's book *The Tech Diet for Your Child & Teen*, which provides a much more comprehensive seven-step plan of action for any family. One of the key areas covered is managing the home WiFi router and smartphone data, both of which control internet connection and online use. By reducing the internet connection you can disable many of the persuasive design and dopamine elements delivered through the devices. Most parents will read that and think, 'Are these guys nuts? We can't turn the home WiFi off when we have established that WFH and hybrid are here to stay.' Don't panic. There are 'mesh router' systems sold worldwide that allow you to create profiles for different people in the house and connect their devices to that profile. If set up correctly, you can have a button to turn off the kids' WiFi at bedtime and leave yours on. In chapter 2, we encouraged you to steer towards hardware solutions over software solutions. This is an example of a hardware solution for the kids and family.

Have fun in the sun!

Ever read that quote, 'You only get 18 summers, make them count'? The message is that the time we have with our kids is precious and fleeting — blink and you'll miss it. We would argue that today you'll probably get only 12 to 14 summers because most teenagers, once they hit their individuation stage, don't want to be seen dead with their uncool parents, let alone be dragged along on a family holiday.

If you're a parent, this may be one of your motivations to rein in busy idiot behaviours. Modelling a healthy work/life balance and being more present during family activities may just be the best gift you can give your kids.

Family life: work to live or live to work — it's your call

1. **Your home is your castle**

   - It should be a sanctuary from work, school, and outside noise and pressures.

   - Busy idiots increasingly, if unintentionally, blur the line between work and family life, letting work invade their castle.

   - This can have profound impacts on your health and wellbeing.

 Top tip: Build a moat around your castle and don't let work spill into your home life.

2. **Be more present at home**

   - Implement a sustainable audit and harvest trees.

   - Downtime should be relaxing; make sure work or personal tech doesn't disrupt your flow.

   - Think of family meals and activities, and connecting with friends, as face-to-face opportunities for oxytocin release.

   - Sleep and exercise are crucial to human function. Don't let busy idiot habits encroach on them.

Top tip: Set up your home office with cues that indicate a clear transition between work mode and family mode.

3. How to quell the uprising: kids and technology

- Children and teens breaking screen time and phone rules is one of the top stressors parents experience at home.

- Most kids aren't ready to self-regulate their screen time. It's not a personal attack on your parenting—it's science.

- Target the home WiFi and smartphone data limits as a first step.

- For a more complex family intervention, check out Brad's book *The Tech Diet for Your Child & Teen*.

Top tip: Model a healthy work/life balance and being more present during family activities—it may just be the best gift you can give your kids.

Conclusion

Imagine a world free of Busy Idiots?

Sadly, most people aren't happy at work. In our home country, according to the Indeed/YouGov 2022 Workplace Happiness Survey, 72 per cent of employed Australians have felt unhappy at work over the past year. Australia is nicknamed 'the lucky country' for its beautiful beaches and landscapes, warm weather, and wealth of natural resources and employment opportunities. The unemployment rate is low (3.8 per cent as of April 2024). If people are miserable at work here, God knows how people must be feeling trudging into their corporate job through the sleet on a frigid winter's morning in the UK. In the US, the mood may be even worse: in a recent Gallup survey, 80 per cent of Americans reported being dissatisfied with how things are going across the board. What's going on?

Some older commentators argue that we're too self-entitled these days, that we don't know how good we've got it! 'In my day…' they will begin. 'Shut up, suit up and show up!' seems to be the message. We need to embrace a stoical mindset and recognise the benefits of developing resilience. It's true that our working conditions have never been better. We're grateful that we get to work from a comfortable home studio or office and not down a mine, or worse, in a theatre of war as our grandparents did. But it's too simplistic to argue that somehow today's workers have evolved to be softer than 50-plus years ago. No, that's not the answer. Time moves on and working conditions in western societies have improved. Yet, a comfortable, safe working environment should be a minimum expectation, not a cause for celebration.

Most companies run an employee engagement survey at least once a year; more progressive companies run them far more regularly. These surveys normally ask big questions, such as, 'How satisfied are you with your current role and responsibilities?' or 'How well do you feel supported by your manager/ supervisor?', rated on a Likert scale, from 1 — very dissatisfied to 5 — very satisfied. They will usually include a box for open-ended comments. (Very few companies take our advice from chapter 5 — 'Genchi Genbutsu' followed up with qualitative interviews to find out what's really going on.) An employee satisfaction (or 'engagement') number is spat out and HR and the leadership celebrate if the figure is trending upward or panic if it's trending downward (HR leaders' KPIs are sometimes tied to this score). What follows is a hypothesis-led conversation about how business leaders can improve employee engagement. We hope they do this because they care about their employees' welfare, but it's also good for business. The data is clear and unsurprising, showing that more highly engaged teams deliver better business results. (According to a 2022 survey by HR Cloud, a highly engaged workforce increases profitability by 21 per cent.) These hypotheses usually take a micro, short-term view of what's going on in the current business context. Numbers have to be hit month by month, quarter by quarter, so leaders need a quick turnaround in employee engagement. The hypotheses that are being discussed in most leadership meetings globally in 2024 include, 'Working from home is ruining our employee engagement; let's get everyone back!' and 'Let's do more face-to-face team building'. We'd argue that these actions are largely red herrings and don't address the true causes of employee unhappiness that have been bubbling away for decades.

What is the problem then?

Busyness, or rather our obsession with busyness, is the biggest, yet still unspoken issue in the modern workplace. There are many factors that cause stress, burnout, loneliness and overall unhappiness. As human beings, we intrinsically crave control. We want to feel that we are safe and in control of our own lives. Busyness prevents that.

We've outlined how technology can work against you to steal your attention and keep you distracted. Brad has spent more than 20 years helping address screen addiction; he might be the most prominent expert in the country on this topic. Yet, the hypocrisy was staring him in the face. Busy parents would pay for their children to get help, and time after time struggle to pay attention to his advice, because they were as distracted as their children! For some reason, it's fine for adults to be addicted to screens but not their children. Do as I say, not as I do has never been an effective parenting strategy.

We hope this book has given you practical tips that will help you harvest technology. Don't beat yourself up if you can't action everything all at once. Small, incremental progress is still progress. Every hour you get back from unwanted screen usage is an hour you can spend doing meaningful work or for time with your friends or family, or doing something fun or doing nothing at all! Remember, we encourage you to do nothing sometimes — it's the ultimate f*ck-you to busyness.

While technology can work against you, you might also have a busy boss in your grill! Both steal your focus, pointing you in all the wrong directions, leaving you feeling unsatisfied, lost and trapped. Our aim is to help you take back control of your day-to-day life and your career. Not everything we've suggested will work for you. Experiment to find out what works best and hone the techniques.

If you're thinking around now, 'Oh my God, I'm a busy boss!', congratulations for your excellent self-awareness. That's a great leadership skill, and it shows you have empathy (another key leadership trait, which we outlined in chapter 6). So don't beat yourself up. As we've outlined, busyness is an unhealthy sickness within corporations, but it's never too late for either you or the organisation to get better, and chapter 5 offered plenty of tips on how to do this.

Remember the old adage (attributed to Christopher McCandless) that happiness is only real when shared. When you catch up with former colleagues who have become friends, what do you talk about? Do you revisit the operating model you redesigned? Or reminisce about that marketing plan that came off and grew sales by 10 per cent. Of course you don't. You talk about the people, the camaraderie, the laughs and the tears. Simply, you talk about the human connections and emotions you experienced together.

Today, more than ever, people are questioning their career choices until it becomes a source of anxiety. Do I really want to be an accountant all my life? How did I become a risk and resilience specialist? Such questions are normal; doubt is the thinking person's friend. Take solace in the fact that whatever you do, you work with people. A tennis player might be alone on the court, but off-court she has a team of supporters behind her. No matter what industry you work in, having fun with the people you work with will improve your happiness. It's hard to have fun at work, though, if you're not part of a productive, successful team. The toolkit in chapter 5 outlined practical ways you can form productive and happy teams — teams that get their work done but don't burn the midnight oil.

Finally, work is just work. This doesn't mean you shouldn't care about your job; of course you should. If, however, your work defines you, if it is your primary identity, it's time to slow down and reflect on what is truly important in your life. By all means take pride in your work and career, but don't become obsessive. The more you obsess, the more work you'll find to do; it's the path to busyness. Remember the law of least effort: the less I do, the more I achieve. Don't make the mistake of waiting until you're retired to start enjoying your life. You have permission to enjoy your life every single day. Chapter 6 provides a toolkit for creating your castle and protecting your family and personal life.

Why did you have to call us idiots?

Sorry about that! By now, we hope you'll have understood that we're all busy idiots to some extent some of the time. We have both lost many days being busy idiots and sadly we know we'll lose more in the future. It happens. We gave this book its abrasive title out of a sense of frustration. It's a call to arms, shouted from the rooftops: stop doing it! As we've discussed, modern workplaces recognise many issues, including loneliness, burnout, engagement, satisfaction, wellbeing, safety, diversity, equity, inclusion, security, fairness. The list is endless! But busyness? No, that's taboo! We're *supposed* to be busy, it's a *good* thing. We'll end with this to drive our point home. What words are typically exchanged at the start of most introductory meetings?

'Hi Simon, nice to meet you. How are you?'

'Yeah, really busy at the moment. How about you?'

'Flat out, really busy too! I guess it's that *time of year!'*

It's always that time of year. What if there was a world where it was not only acceptable but applauded to *not* be busy? A world where busyness, rather than being a badge of honour, was seen as a sign you're not coping. A world where you had no fear your boss would interpret your lack of busyness as a green light to load you up with more work or, worse, make you redundant.

Take a minute to picture in your mind sitting down at your next meeting with your boss. Got it in your head? Now picture this exchange:

Boss: 'So how are you going?'

You: 'I'm fantastic thanks, not busy at all.'

Get in touch

We like to consider ourselves as friendly humans who love to connect. If you have a workplace frozen by busyness reach out!

- **Visit:** www.busyidiots.net

- **Instagram:** @busyidiots

- **LinkedIn:** Joff Outlaw, Brad Marshall

Or follow the QR code for more busy buster resources.

References

Introduction

Dahlgreen, W. (2015) *37% of British workers think their jobs are meaningless, YouGov.* Available at: https://yougov.co.uk/society/articles/13005-british-jobs-meaningless (Accessed: 29 July 2024).

Chapter 1

Kätsyri, J, Hari, R, Ravaja, N, & Nummenmaa, L (2013). The opponent matters: elevated FMRI reward responses to winning against a human versus a computer opponent during interactive video game playing. *Cerebral cortex 23*(12), 2829–39. https://doi.org/10.1093/cercor/bhs259

Chapter 3

Clifton, J, & Harter, J (2019). *It's the Manager.* Gallup.

Hatt, RM, Dunn, HC, Tiernan, RL, & Tiger, JH (2022). Evaluating the effects of scheduled breaks on undergraduate school productivity. Public Library of Science. *Journal of Applied Behavior Analysis*, EJ13364575, May 11.

Carnegie, D (1936). *How to Win Friends and Influence People.* Simon & Schuster, New York.

Chapter 4

Yuhan, C, Mingming, L, Fu, G, & Xueshuang, W (2023). The effect of short-form video addiction on users' attention. *Behaviour & Information Technology 42*(16), 2893–910.

Shockley, KM, Gabriel, AS, Robertson, D, Rosen, CC, et al. (2021). The fatiguing effects of camera use in virtual meetings: A within-person field experiment. *Journal of Applied Psychology 106*(8), 1137.

Bennett, AA, Campion, ED, Keeler, KR, & Keener, SK (2021). Videoconference fatigue? Exploring changes in fatigue after videoconference meetings during COVID-19. *Journal of Applied Psychology 106*(3), 330.

Blanchard, AL (2021). The effects of COVID-19 on virtual working within online groups. *Group Processes & Intergroup Relations 24*(2), 290–6.

Tomprou, M, Kim, YJ, Chikersal, P, Woolley, AW, et al. (2021). Speaking out of turn: How video conferencing reduces vocal synchrony and collective intelligence. *PLoS ONE 16*(3): e0247655. https://doi.org/10.1371/journal.pone.0247655

Gruber, J, Hargittai, E, & Nguyen, MH (2022). The value of face-to-face communication in the digital world: What people miss about in-person interactions when those are limited. *Studies in Communication Sciences,* 1–19. https://doi.org/10.24434/j.scoms.2022.03.3340

Kordova, S, & Hirschprung, RS (2023). Effectiveness of the forced usage of alternative digital platforms during the COVID-19 pandemic in project communication management. *Heliyon 9*(11).

Kahlow, J, Klecka, H, & Ruppel, E (2020). What the differences in conflict between online and face-to-face work groups mean for hybrid groups: A state-of-the-art review. *Review of Communication Research 8*, 51–77. https://doi.org/10.12840/ISSN.2255-4165.023

Lim, MH, & Smith, B (2023). *State of the Nation Report: Social Connections in Australia 2023.*

Chapter 6

Paulus, MP, Squeglia, LM, Bagot, K, & Jacobus, J, et al. (2019). Screen media activity and brain structure in youth: Evidence for diverse structural correlation networks from the ABCD study. *NeuroImage 185,* 140–53. https://doi.org/10.1016/j.neuroimage.2018.10.040

Conclusion

Gallup (2022) *Satisfaction with the United States, Gallup.com.* Available at: https://news.gallup.com/poll/1669/general-mood-country.aspx (Accessed: 29 July 2024).